Perfect Days

DUBLIN

Travel with
**Insider
Tips**

www.marco-polo.com

Contents

 TOP 10   4

That Dublin Feeling   6

For chapters: See inside front cover

TOP 10

Not to be missed!
Our TOP 10 hits – from the absolute No. 1 to No. 10 –
help you plan your tour of the most important sights.

⭐1 TRINITY COLLEGE & THE *BOOK OF KELLS* ➤ 92

The illuminated gospel is Ireland's most beautiful book, one that has been included in UNESCO's Memory of the World Register, ensuring its number 1 position in the TOP 10.

⭐2 NATIONAL MUSEUM OF IRELAND – ARCHAEOLOGY ➤ 98

This impressive building houses two million exhibits, including valuable Celtic prehistoric artefacts.

⭐3 KILMAINHAM GAOL ➤ 58

The 200-year-old prison is of interest for its architecture but also, more importantly, for its history. Many of the leaders who shaped Ireland's history were incarcerated inside its walls.

⭐4 GUINNESS STOREHOUSE ➤ 61

An interesting brewery museum that showcases the history of Guinness from a small Irish family business to a global brand.

⭐5 ST PATRICK'S CATHEDRAL ➤ 65

Ireland's largest church is dedicated to Saint Patrick, the country's patron saint, and the building embodies one thousand years of Irish history.

⭐6 TEMPLE BAR ➤ 68

This is the city's social heart: a vibrant district of pubs, cafes, shops and restaurants, colourful town houses, cobbled streets and authentic Irish flair (➤ left).

⭐7 NATIONAL GALLERY OF IRELAND ➤ 101

Housed in a Renaissance-style mansion this impressive collection boasts works by both European Old Masters and important Irish artists such as Jack B Yeats.

⭐8 PHOENIX PARK ➤ 126

A peaceful urban park that is an impressive example of the Irish love for gardens, plants and greenery, and for Dubliners it adds a good deal to the quality of life in the city.

⭐9 DUBLIN CASTLE ➤ 70

Once a medieval castle, then a Georgian palace, this was for centuries the stronghold of English rule in Ireland. Visitors can now view the staterooms and apartments once used by the British viceroys.

⭐10 ST STEPHEN'S GREEN ➤ 104

Monuments and statutes, trees and plants from around the world, small ponds and lakes – the magnificent city park is a green oasis surrounded by grand Georgian town houses.

THAT
DUBLIN

Experience the city's unique flair and find out what makes it tick – just like the Dubliners themselves.

DRAMA, COMEDY AND MAGIC

The repertoire of the **Gaiety Theatre** (► 36) is just as multifaceted as life itself – or so its fans say – and performances are often sold out. It comes as no surprise that Dubliners know all of the actors who perform here and eagerly await new reviews. You may need a little luck if you want to buy tickets for the popular classics so your best bet is to book well in advance.

TIME FOR A PINT

The legendary **O'Donoghue's** (► 119) is usually bursting at the seams. Enjoy the jovial atmosphere and live music and try some of the many different varieties of beer and cider on offer. Quite a few of the Irish that emigrated come back here to take part in the impromptu sessions of Irish folk songs.

IN JOYCE'S FOOTSTEPS

Sweny's (✚ 192 B2) is where Leopold Bloom bought his lemon-scented soap on 16 June 1904 in James Joyce's *Ulysses*. Opened in the mid-19th century, the pharmacy is now a museum, second-hand bookshop and meeting place for fans and scholars of literature, who come for the daily readings of Joyce's works (Lincoln Place 1, D2, Mon–Sat 11–5, readings Mon–Fri 1pm, Thu also 7pm, Sat 11am, free entry; www.sweny.ie).

LUNCH LIKE THE IRISH

Dublin's cafes and restaurants are often busy at lunchtime and tables are hard to come by so as a lovely alternative why not grab some tasty treats and join the locals for a picnic on the grass at **St Stephen's Green** (► 104). Sit right down next to the office workers and tourists enjoying their sandwiches and have a chat and take in the sunshine and natural surroundings instead.

APPLE PIE ON A PALLADIAN MANSION TERRACE

For a getaway Dubliners need only take a 45-minute city bus ride to the little country village of Enniskerry surrounded by the Wicklow Mountains. The village is the starting point for a charming

FEELING

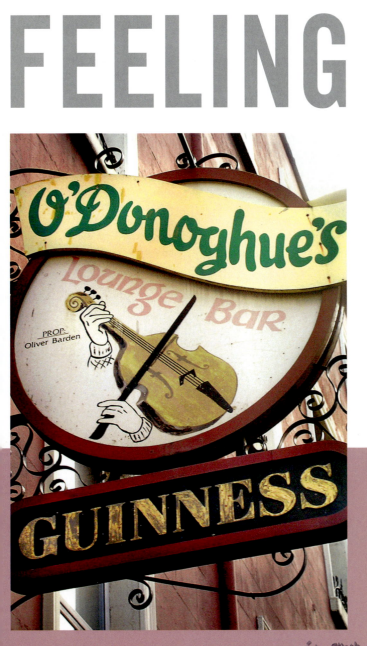

The famous O'Donoghue's near St Stephen's Green

That Dublin Feeling

walk to the magnificent **Powerscourt Estate** (► 150) where you will find a self-service restaurant and tearoom. Take a seat in the Terrace Cafe's teak furniture and enjoy the delightful views of the landscaped park – and share some gardening tips with the locals.

SUNDAY STREET ART

A stroll around the Open Air Art Gallery on **Merrion Square** (► 111) is a Sunday must for Dublin's art lovers. The "gallery" is a collection of simple street stands – as many as 200 on fine days in summer – where artists display their work on the fence around the square or propped up on the pavement. Take your time and chat to the artists about their work. The atmosphere is relaxed and rather jovial.

LUXURY DEPARTMENT STORE WITH DESIGNER BRANDS

Tradition, Irish products and exquisite quality: **Brown Thomas** (► 117) is Dublin's answer to Harrods. This is where mothers bring their daughters to shop for their trousseaux, or to choose the perfect ball gown for the next season, or a tasteful tweed business suit, or just to catch up on the latest Irish design trends. Once you've done your shopping you can take a break in one of the department store's two cafes.

THE SOUND OF THE SEA, THE CRIES OF THE GULLS

Regardless of where you are in Howth (at the harbour, or on the steep cliffs high above the town, or on a walk from the Baily Lighthouse to Howth Head) it's immediately clear that **Howth** (► 33) is the most picturesque of Dublin's seaside suburbs. Dubliners not only flock here to eat in the rustic seafood restaurants but also to go golfing and sailing. Those with an interest in the spiritual – and there are quite a few – visit Aideen's Grave, a megalith tomb in the grounds of Howth Castle, believed to be a place of special power. It takes just 20 minutes to get from Dublin to Howth on the DART.

Baily Lighthouse on Howth Head

The Magazine

DUBLIN
today

There's no denying that Dublin has come of age. Local writer Brendan Behan once described the city as "the largest village in Europe", while for James Joyce, "dear dirty Dublin" was the key to understanding all the cities of the world. In many ways both were right.

Today's "fair city" oozes confidence as the increasingly fashionable capital of a young, independent, democratic republic no longer living on its Georgian past and dominated by the puritanical spirit of Irish Catholicism. Over the years it has been reinvented by U2, Colin Farrell, Roddy Doyle and Riverdance to become a fun-loving, consciously European city, abuzz with sophisticated bars, restaurants, clubs and shops, as well as world-class museums and galleries. "City of a thousand pubs and a thousand bands", "capital of Euro-cool", "The Literary Giant", "party capital of

Europe" – the list of epithets goes on. No wonder Dublin is one of Europe's favourite holiday destinations, in spite of recent economic troubles.

Vibrant Commercial Centre

The capital's transformation was mainly due to its rapid economic development. From 1994 until the downturn began to bite in 2007, the Irish economy sustained an average annual growth of more than 7 per cent – the highest in the European Union – prompting the British journal *The Economist* to coin the term "Celtic Tiger". Dublin developed into a world-class banking centre, the London–Dublin air route became the fourth busiest in the world and, with Ireland as the world's second largest exporter of software, the government strove to establish the city as the e-commerce capital of Europe. The success of the Celtic Tiger, combined with the youngest population in Europe (40 per cent are under 25 years of age) and the huge growth in the number of immigrants and visitors, led to increased prosperity.

Boom and Bust

The bubble burst with the collapse of the world economy in 2008–2009. By early 2010 Ireland's GDP had contracted by 14 per cent, and by the end of that year its economy had collapsed, resulting in a €67.5 billion bailout by the EU and IMF. The economy started to pick up again at the end of 2013 and Ireland was able to leave the EU rescue package and

Dublin's Docklands at dusk with the Samuel Beckett Bridge designed by Santiago Calatrava (2009) spanning the Liffey

return to the capital market and obtain fresh financing without any problems. This was followed by rapid economic recovery, The Irish economy expanded by 4 per cent in 2015 and the gross domestic product grew by an enormous 7 per cent (the highest in the European Union) after an already more-than-respectable 5.2 per cent in the year before. Unemployment and the national debt are continuing to decrease and the banks are also gradually getting back on their feet.

Legacy of the Celtic Tiger

Despite the economic downturn, Dublin's period of boom changed it irreversibly. You have only to walk the streets to see the modern architecture and the extraordinary number of new hotels, pubs and restaurants in both new and restored buildings. The downside of Dublin's economic miracle was a dramatic rise in prices and traffic congestion.

> "You can still find a quiet pub to while away a few hours"

Ironically for a nation with a tradition of emigration, the capital is only slowly getting to grips with its nascent multi-culturalism, following the dramatic influx of immigrants.

The Pygmalion Café at Powerscourt Townhouse shopping complex

Dublin's James Joyce Bridge, built during the heyday of the Celtic Tiger

Enduring Traditions

The new Dublin has been careful not to replace the old Dublin. The city has reinvented itself but also retained its inimitable character, carefully preserving everything that makes it unique. With its clever blend of urban dynamism and small-town informality and charm, there is still nowhere quite like it.

The essence of the Irish capital and its people hasn't really changed: the Dubliners' well-deserved reputation for friendliness, wit and irrepressible sense of fun remains. You can still find a quiet pub in the heart of the city, where you can while away a few hours; and if you are lucky, traditional musicians will be playing for free. Alternatively, wander through the back streets and take pleasure in the classical symmetry of an elegant Georgian square, or admire the views along the Liffey quays. When you stop for refreshment, you'll still find traditional Irish dishes among the more inventive options that feature on Dublin's menus; and Guinness is still good for you!

Perhaps the most subtle change is the emergence of a new breed of Dubliners – typically young, confident and well-educated – who have realized their worth on the world market. Their powerful pride of place is almost tangible; their love of Dublin remains constant no matter how much the city changes.

Historic **DUBLIN**

Since its origins as a Gaelic settlement over 1,000 years ago, Dublin has travelled a turbulent road, assailed by Viking raiders, Norman conquerors and English settlers, and then suffering decades of rebellions and war before finding peace and independence.

Gaelic origins and Viking Settlement

The Irish-Gaelic name for Dublin today, *Ath Cliath*, or Ford of the Hurdles, refers to the first Gaelic settlement established upstream from the present city. Viking raiders arrived in the ninth century, attracted by the Liffey's wide opening to the sea, and established a trading settlement called *Dubh Linn*, derived from the Irish for "black pool". This was a dark pool of water where the River Poddle entered the River Liffey. The Danes maintained control of Dublin until 1171 when Dermot MacMurrough of Leinster captured the city with the aid of an Anglo-Norman army.

Norman Dublin

The arrival of the Anglo-Normans changed the political landscape of Ireland forever. The Norman occupation and their attempted conquest of the country were controlled from Dublin. By 1400 many of the Norman conquerors had been absorbed into Irish society and had adopted Irish language and culture. This left only a heavily defended area around Dublin, known as The Pale, under direct English control.

Elizabethan and Georgian Dublin

In the 16th and 17th centuries Dublin and its people were transformed under Tudor rule. The "Old English" families of The Pale supported the complete conquest of Ireland and disarmament of the native Irish, but they were almost exclusively Roman Catholic and the ravages of the Reformation in England began to alienate them.

In 1592 Elizabeth I opened Trinity College (➤ 92) as a Protestant University for the Irish gentry. Many important Dublin families spurned Trinity and instead sent their sons to Catholic universities in Europe. In turn, Elizabeth viewed the "Old English" of Dublin as unreliable and encouraged the settlement of Protestant "New English", who formed the basis for English administration in Ireland until the 19th century.

By the beginning of the 18th century the English had established complete control of Ireland and imposed Penal Laws on the Roman Catholic majority. In Dublin, the Protestant Ascendancy thrived and undertook a building programme, replacing the city's narrow medieval alleys with wide Georgian streets and squares. Only the narrow streets around Temple Bar (➤ 68) and Grafton Street (➤ 109) survived.

Despite these opulent buildings, 18th-century Dublin was marked by desperate poverty, exacerbated by rural migration. The migration affected the demographics of the city, with Catholics again becoming the majority.

From Rebellion to Civil War

Dublin did not reap the full benefits of the 19th-century industrial revolution; instead it was left with thousands of unskilled, unemployed poor, a situation blamed on British policy in Ireland. Fuelled by radical political thinking and a Gaelic revival, a new revolutionary organization called the Irish Republican Brotherhood or Fenians was formed in 1867. It attempted an armed insurrection to end British rule in Ireland, and although this failed the seed of armed rebellion was sown.

In 1916, many young Dublin men were away fighting for the British in World War I, lured by the promise of home rule for Ireland when the "emergency" was over. At home, others acted on the old saying, "England's difficulty is Ireland's opportunity", and organized a rising for Easter 1916. Armed units of the Irish Volunteers and the Irish Citizen Army occupied major buildings. During their week-long siege, many citizens and soldiers were killed and there was widespread looting and destruction.

Independence and Regeneration

During the War of Independence (1918–21) and the Civil War (1921–22) Dublin stagnated. It fared better than most Irish cities during the Irish Free State (1922–49) and the new Republic of Ireland from 1949, but struggled economically and was run down. Georgian Dublin began to disappear, as whole streets were replaced with uninspiring office blocks. It wasn't until the 1980s that the outlook changed. Preservation orders came into place, and parts of Dublin got a makeover, mainly between St Stephen's Green and Temple Bar. The Celtic Tiger had more far-reaching effects with the construction of new bridges, cultural sites, designer apartments and offices, culminating in the regeneration of the Docklands and the new Aviva Stadium on the site of Lansdowne Road.

Door knocker on a Georgian house in Merrion Square (left); the General Post Office, the headquarters of the Irish Volunteers during the Easter Rising of 1916 (right)

POETS & STORYTELLERS

Considering its small size, Dublin has produced more than its fair share of celebrated writers. Three Nobel Prizes for literature have been awarded to its progeny.

Dublin's Nobel Laureates are George Bernard Shaw, William Butler Yeats and Samuel Beckett – and there have been numerous other luminaries. Dublin's writing tradition, nurtured for centuries in the nicotine-stained bars, seems to infiltrate every corner of the city. As soon as you arrive, the ghosts of James Joyce, Brendan Behan and Oscar Wilde sweep you along on a tide of literary consciousness – with Dublin's overcrowded bars, colloquial conversations, decaying tenements and Georgian facades as stage sets for the city's larger-than-life drama.

Left: The Oscar Wilde statue in Merrion Square. Right: WB Yeats

The Irish literary tradition dates back to early Gaelic civilizations, through troubadour songs and manuscripts preserved by monks and poets. The *Book of Kells*, (▶96), with its elaborate illuminations, is an exceptional example of Ireland's early reverence for words.

Rich Heritage

The first great Irish writer in English was the satirist Jonathan Swift (▶20), a graduate of Trinity College and author of the allegorical *Gulliver's Travels* (1726). George Farquhar (*c.* 1677–1707), a contemporary of Swift, sacrificed acting to become a playwright after accidentally wounding a fellow actor with a sword. His most successful restoration comedies, *The Beaux Stratagem* and *The Recruiting Officer*, are still popular today. In the mid-19th century, novelists Joseph Sheridan Le Fanu (1814–73) and Bram Stoker (1847–1912),

LITERARY PUBS

- Brendan Behan and Patrick Kavanagh used to frequent the **Duke** (▶91).
- **McDaid's** (▶120 and 164) was popular with Behan, Kavanagh and Flann O'Brien. It was also a setting for James Joyce's short story *Grace*.
- Flann O'Brien was also a patron of **Neary's** (▶164).
- **The Stag's Head** (▶163) was a regular haunt of Joyce.
- **Toner's** (▶119 and 164) was the only pub William Butler Yeats ever entered.
- **Davy Byrne's** (▶119 and 164) was where Joyce's hero Bloom had a gorgonzola cheese sandwich and a glass of burgundy for lunch in *Ulysses*.

Left: Illustration, *Gulliver's Travels*

Right: James Joyce statue, Merrion Hotel courtyard

both Dublin-born, came to the fore with their new genre of horror. After his wife died in 1858, Le Fanu became a recluse. He wrote his most famous works, *Uncle Silas* and *The House by the Churchyard*, in bed between the hours of midnight and dawn in an attempt to exorcize his obsession with death and the supernatural.

Inspired by Le Fanu, Stoker began his literary career as an unpaid drama critic on the *Dublin Evening Mail*. His masterwork, *Dracula*, was moderately well received but following its posthumous dramatization in 1924 it became a resounding success.

Sophistication to Nationalism

Nineteenth-century refinement could be observed in the sophisticated social plays of George Bernard Shaw (▶ 79), including *Pygmalion*, *Saint Joan and Arms and the Man*; and in those of Irish wit, poet and dramatist Oscar Wilde (▶ 111), whose worldwide fame rests on such comic masterpieces as *Lady Windermere's Fan*, *An Ideal Husband* and *The Importance of Being Earnest*. These two Dublin-born playwrights created works

The back yard and the door knocker at the George Bernard Shaw Birthplace

that dominated the theatre on both sides of the Irish Sea from the 1880s until World War II. This period marked the Golden Age of Dublin literature, and Shaw was awarded the Nobel Prize for literature in 1925. But it was WB Yeats (1865–1939), a member of the Irish Free State Senate and the Irish Republican Brotherhood (a forerunner of the IRA) who best captured the restless, yearning spirit of Irish nationalism in such plays as *Cathleen ni Houlihan* and the poem *Easter 1916*, with its immortal line "All changed, changed utterly: a terrible beauty is born". Yeats' reputation rests more on his poetry, for which he received the Nobel Prize for literature in 1923. Yeats hailed Sean O'Casey (1880–1964) as a literary genius. His first plays – *The Shadow of a Gunman*, *Juno and the Paycock* and *The Plough and the Stars* – showed how

> "It was WB Yeats who best captured the restless yearning spirit of Irish nationalism"

the real victims of the civil war had been the civilians. They proved too close for comfort for many, and audiences rioted at their premières.

Capturing Dublin

James Joyce (1882–1941) celebrated the character of Dublin more than any other Irish author, in works such as *The Dubliners*, *A Portrait of the Artist as a Young Man* and, his finest achievement, the epic *Ulysses*.

Other protégés of post-war Dublin include Joyce's friend, the Nobel Prize-winning dramatist, novelist Samuel Beckett (▶ 95); poet Patrick Kavanagh; and Brendan Behan, author, anti-English rebel and alcoholic from the age of eight. Popular novelists include CS Lewis, Edna O'Brien, Flann O'Brien, JP Donleavy, Maeve Binchy and Booker Prize-winners Roddy Doyle and John Banville, all of whom have immortalized aspects of Ireland in their best-selling books. Dublin tourist information offices also have a free map and brochure called *City of Words – Dublin's Literary Attractions* showing the city's literary highlights, for more information visit www.dublincityofliterature.ie

PEOPLE &
POLITICS

No visitor can escape the haunting presence of the men and women who shaped Dublin's and the country's history. Their memory lives on everywhere in the city, in its place names and its monuments.

St Patrick (Fifth Century)

Christianity first came to Ireland around the beginning of the fifth century with the arrival of St Patrick, the patron saint of Ireland who, according to legend, rid the country of snakes. He is said to have used the shamrock, with its leaf divided into three, to illustrate the oneness of the Holy Trinity. The shamrock has become the national emblem of Ireland.

Jonathan Swift (1667–1745)

Satirist, political journalist and churchman, Jonathan Swift was Dean of St Patrick's Cathedral from 1713 to 1745, during which time he became a fierce advocate for the economic rights of the Irish people. Many of his best-known works were written during this time, including his greatest satire, *Gulliver's Travels*, often regarded as a children's book but in fact one of the most powerful exposés of human folly ever penned.

Theobald Wolfe Tone (1763–98)

This radical Protestant lawyer and "Father of Irish Republicanism" founded the United Irishmen in 1791, and staged illegal meetings in the Tailor's Hall (▶ 75). It is thought that their unsuccessful 1798 revolt helped convince the British Government to impose the Act of Union and direct rule from London.

Arthur Guinness (1725–1803)

Arthur Guinness was just 34 when he acquired the small, disused Rainsford's Ale Brewery in St James's Gate in 1759 and started black-roasting malt to produce Guinness (▶ 61). Today, his legacy persists in the heady malt and hop smells that waft across Dublin, and in the Guinness consumed in more than 120 countries worldwide every day.

Arthur Wellesley, First Duke of Wellington (1769–1852)

Arthur Wellesley was born into an Anglo-Irish landowning family. His precise birthplace is uncertain but it seems likely to have been Dublin. After a childhood spent between County Meath, Dublin and Eton in England, he gained a commission in the British army, serving in Ireland and India, as well as becoming involved in politics. Wellesley is best known for his role in the Peninsular Wars and the Battle of Waterloo, which gained him his dukedom. He became Conservative Prime Minster twice and oversaw the emancipation of Catholics in Great Britain and Ireland.

Daniel O'Connell (1775–1847)

Known as "the Liberator", Daniel O'Connell was a brilliant politician, lawyer and orator who secured Catholic emancipation for Ireland in 1829, rallying support through enormous, non-violent mass meetings. Sadly, his peaceful methods were not successful in gaining Home Rule for the Irish, but his

Mary Robinson, the first female president (1990–97) of the Republic of Ireland

achievements earned him an eternal place in Dubliners' hearts and in Dublin's main street (➤ 130), now named after him.

Countess Markievicz (1868–1927)

In 1908, Countess Constance Markievicz, a member of the Anglo-Irish landed gentry class, became committed to the nationalist cause and joined Sinn Féin (a national political party in Ireland). A key figure in the 1916 Easter Rising (➤ 58), she escaped execution on account of her public status and gender. In 1918 she became the first woman to be elected to the British House of Commons but, in keeping with Sinn Féin's policy, she refused to take her seat.

James Larkin (1876–1947)

Liverpool-born "Big Jim" Larkin, the great trade unionist, changed the lives of thousands of unskilled Dublin labourers who, in the early 20th century, worked and lived in some of the worst conditions in Europe. Their employers ordered them to sign a declaration that they would not join Larkin's Irish Transport and General Workers Union. This led to the "Dublin lock-out," from August 1913 to February 1914, during which many thousands of workers went on strike, there were violent confrontations between police and strikers, and the city ground to a standstill. Although the strike was ultimately unsuccessful, it forced a new era in industrial relations.

Mary Robinson (born 1944)

Mary Robinson, a liberal lawyer and graduate of Trinity College, became the first woman president of the Republic of Ireland in 1990. Seven years later she relinquished the presidency to take on the role of United Nations High Commissioner for Human Rights. She was succeeded by Mary McAleese, who served two terms before being replaced by Michael Higgins.

The Shaping of a Nation

Key figures in the 1916 Easter Rising included union organizer James Connolly; poet Pádraic Pearse, leader of Irish nationalism, who proclaimed Ireland's independence from Britain from the steps of the General Post Office; Michael Collins, head of the Irish Volunteers' campaign of urban guerrilla warfare; and Éamon de Valera, the motivator of the Irish Republican Army (IRA).

Left to right: Revolutionary Michael Collins (1890–1922); Collins' tomb in Glasnevin Cemetery; Enda Kenny, elected Taoiseach in 2011

All were imprisoned at Kilmainham Gaol (➤ 58). As General of the Irish Free State Army during the Irish War of Independence, Michael Collins was part of the delegation that shaped the Anglo-Irish Treaty in 1921 and was thus held partly responsible for the creation of Northern Ireland. He was killed in 1922 during the Irish Civil War that followed. De Valera went on to lead his country through its final severance with Britain during a 16-year term as Taoiseach (see below), and in 1959 became the president of Ireland.

Taoiseachs

Pronounced "Tee-shock", Taoiseach is the Irish name for the head of government in Ireland, a role appointed by the president. After the Irish War of Independence ended with the Anglo-Irish Treaty in 1922, there were two presidents of the Executive Council before Éamon de Valera took the title of Taoiseach, a role he held three times between 1937 and 1957. Other well-known figures to hold the title include Garret Fitzgerald (1981–87), who signed the Anglo-Irish Agreement in 1985, outlining a closer relationship between the Republic of Ireland and Great Britain on matters regarding Northern Ireland.

By the time Bertie Ahern became Taoiseach in 1997, the period of growth that gave rise to the Celtic Tiger moniker was at its peak. One of his main achievements was to oversee the Good Friday Agreement that worked towards peace in Northern Ireland. In 2011, Fine Gael leader Enda Kenny was elected as Taoiseach.

Oysters &

GUINNESS

The past decade or so in Dublin has seen the emergence of a vibrant and cosmopolitan food culture, with dozens of fashionable new restaurants serving global cuisine. Despite the economic downturn, this international outlook is here to stay, but traditional Irish dishes have also undergone a renaissance, with a lighter style and exciting new twists.

In spite of Dublin's culinary revolution, the simple dishes and straightforward flavours of Ireland's traditional country cooking are still evident on many menus. And now that the city has come of age gastronomically it has the self-confidence to be proud of this culinary heritage.

Traditional Irish Cuisine

The appeal of traditional Irish cuisine is its wholesomeness, the cooking of a primarily agricultural society whose main purpose is to nourish and sustain. Fish is a mainstay, together with meat and dairy, a wide range of breads, cakes and puddings, and a well-stocked basket of fresh fruit and vegetables.

Typical Irish dishes commonly found in the capital include the quintessential Irish stew (made with mutton or lamb, onions and potatoes), Dublin coddle (boiled sausages, bacon, onions and potatoes in a thickened sauce), boxties (Irish potato pancakes with various savoury fillings), lamb and seafood (fresh and smoked salmon, Dublin Bay prawns and oysters, which are often consumed with Guinness); baked ham roasted with cloves and brown sugar and commonly served with boiled cabbage; slow-cooked beef and stout casseroles with mountains of fresh vegetables (leeks, carrots, potatoes of every shape, texture and size) and a huge variety of Irish cheeses.

Irish breads and cakes are also especially tasty: try the soda bread, scones and barm brack (a doughy, fruity tea bread), apple tarts and porter cake (a dark fruit cake famous for the inclusion of stout, usually Guinness). Irish coffee (with cream and whiskey) makes a perfect end to any evening.

New Irish Cuisine

The best cooks in the city now favour a lighter, more creative style than is traditionally the case in Irish cooking. The resulting Modern Irish cuisine is more experimental, infusing different flavours, colours and culinary styles, but still using the finest Irish produce and with traditional themes at its heart. Casting your eyes down a Dublin menu, you may find such typical Dublin staples as coddle reborn as a shellfish coddle; or Irish black pudding topped with a scoop of blue cheese and cider sorbet. Guinness may be put to new use as a sabayon, coating a succulent steak, as opposed to being employed in a traditional beef and stout stew; and oysters may be served with rice wine for an Asian slant on a favourite Dublin speciality.

Leading exponents of New Irish cuisine include Michelin-starred Kevin Thornton (➤ 117), Patrick Guilbaud (➤ 116) and Derry Clark (➤ 114). They continue to encourage up-and-coming Irish chefs to pay homage to Irish traditions in their contemporary cuisine and to bring real Irish flavour into Dublin's restaurants.

As they say in Irish, *Blas agus sasamh go bhfaighe tu air* (May you find it both tasty and satisfying)!

TIME FOR A TIPPLE

It is not surprising that the Irish are reputedly fond of a tipple if you consider the fine quality of their native drinks. During your stay, try the following:

- A good **stout**, such as Guinness, Murphy's or Darcy's.
- **Baileys**. One of the most popular liqueurs in the world, it is made from two of Ireland's finest products – whiskey and cream. One variation is a "baby-Guinness" – a shot of Kahlúa with a creamy head of Baileys.
- **Irish Whiskey**. Look out for single malts Jameson, Bushmills and Tullamore Dew, and blended whiskeys like Powers and Paddy. Whiskey is a traditional chaser to a drop of the "black stuff". Stored in oak vats for at least three years, and often considerably longer, Irish whiskey has a smooth and distinctive flavour.

THE DUBLIN
CALENDER

Dubliners love having fun. As a result their social calendar is filled with *fleadh* (festivals; pronounced "flah"), sporting fixtures, religious occasions, cultural events and other good reasons to celebrate. Here are some of the highlights.

There is green everywhere you look on Paddy's Day

Paddy's Day

Throughout the world Irishmen and women join together to celebrate St Patrick's Day, but the biggest festivities are held in Dublin, where an exuberant four-day festival of contemporary and traditional music, song and dance culminates in a spectacular parade, all-night parties and flamboyant firework extravaganzas. Traditionally, everyone wears a shamrock, Ireland's national emblem (➤ 20), but nowadays it seems that anything goes. Some years they even dye the Liffey green!

Ulysses

James Joyce's most celebrated novel, *Ulysses*, modelled on Homer's Odyssey, takes the wanderings of the hero Ulysses and re-enacts them in the fictional hero Leopold Bloom, walking the streets of Dublin on a single day – 16 June, 1904. Much of Joyce's Dublin still exists and, on the same day every year, enthusiastic costumed Joyceans gather to retrace Bloom's steps, starting from the Martello tower in Sandycove where the novel opens. Today the tower houses the James Joyce Museum (➤ 33).

The Magazine

January On the stroke of midnight on New Year's Day (1 January), Dubliners start the year the way they mean to continue…by partying!

February The Six Nations Rugby Tournament (varying Saturdays February to March) is one of the year's great social events, with crowds supporting the "Boys in Green" against England, Wales, Scotland, France and Italy. Also in February is the Dublin Film Festival, of international stature, screening old and classic movies at various cinemas. Details from Dublin Tourism (➤ 41).

March If you could choose just one day to be in Ireland's capital city, it should be St Patrick's Day (17 March, ➤ 26). The Colours Boat Race (mid-March weekend), a rowing race on the Liffey between Trinity College and UCD (University College Dublin), marks the first of several river-centred events in the Dublin calendar.

May The first half of May sees the International Dublin Gay Theatre Festival make its mark with a whole heap of play readings, theatre and comedy.

June 16 June in Dublin is Bloomsday, a quirky day of literary commemoration based on the events in *Ulysses* (➤ 26). June also marks the start of the summer festivals, including the Dublin Port Riverfest, featuring tall ships, music and a market. Details from Dublin Tourism (➤ 41).

July Temple Bar's (➤ 68) summer festivities spread from July into August with street performances, music, and movies in Meeting House Square. There are also fun activities for kids, from dance to visual arts workshops. Staged at the Royal Dublin Society Showgrounds in Ballsbridge, the Dublin Horse Show (end of July) is a premier social and sporting event. It is a magnet for horse-lovers from all over the world.

September Big crowds turn out for the All-Ireland Hurling Final (second Sunday) and the All-Ireland Gaelic Football Final (fourth Sunday), both held at Croke Park (➤ 138).

October A busy month with the Dublin Theatre Festival (first two weeks) and the Dublin Marathon. The main celebration, Samhain (Hallowe'en, 31 October) is one of Dublin's few genuinely Celtic traditions, with a spectacular night-time parade.

November Almost 100 top art galleries gather in the RDS (Royal Dublin Society) to showcase some of their best pieces, giving the public easy access to see (and maybe buy) the work.

December The National Concert Hall's Gala Christmas concert is a hot ticket with carols and other songs on the programme. The Leopardstown Races (26–29 December) are a main event in Dublin's horse-racing calendar.

Dublin
Comedy

From the quips of Oscar Wilde to the one-liners of stand-up comedians and the wit of pub raconteurs, Dubliners have long been celebrated for their cracking sense of humour.

It's hard to know when the Dubliners' gift for humour began but Oscar Wilde certainly helped make it famous with his claim at an American customs desk that "I have nothing to declare but my genius." The Dublin-born writer and poet was the first of many sharp-witted Irish comedians to take the wit, cynicism, satire and absurdly tall tales of the city's bars and pubs to a global audience. Nothing is out of bounds for Irish comedians – religion, war, marriage are all treated with equal irreverence.

Irish Comedy on Television

Dave Allen made his name in the 1960s and 1970s as a hard-drinking, chain-smoking raconteur, a role perfected in his rambling monologues in the British TV series *Dave Allen at Large*. As his career waned, others came in his wake: stand-up comedians such as Sean Hughes, Ed Byrne

Left: Ed Byrne performs. Right: The International Bar, a pub and comedy club

FIVE COMEDY VENUES IN DUBLIN

- **Vicar Street** Catch some of the most renowned stand-up acts here (58–59 Thomas Street, D8; tel: 01 775 5800; www.vicarstreet.com)
- **The International Bar** A very central venue with nightly acts (23 Wicklow Street, D2; tel: 01 677 9250; www.international-bar.com)
- **Capital Comedy Club** Home of Battle of the Axe, right beside the Liffey (Ha'penny Bridge Inn, 42 Wellington Quay, D2; tel: 086 815 6987; www.battleoftheaxe.com)
- **The Button Factory** Great multi-purpose venue in Temple Bar (Temple Bar Music Centre, Curved Street, D2; www.buttonfactory.ie)
- **The Laughter Lounge** Large Northside venue with comedy on Thursday, Friday and Saturday nights (Basement 4–8 Eden Quay, O'Connell Bridge, D1; tel: 01 878 3003; www.laughterlounge.com)

and, more recently, Dara O'Briain. Some moved onto TV, including Dermot Morgan, a Dublin-born and educated comedian best known as Father Ted Crilly in *Father Ted*, the popular situation comedy about a household of Catholic priests. Morgan's career was brought prematurely to an end when he died of a heart attack in 1998.

Continuing Success

Today, comedy is big business in the Irish capital; the city has numerous comedy venues and two comedy festivals – the Vodafone Carnival held in Iveagh Gardens in July and the Bulmers International Comedy Festival in venues across the city in September. But whenever you visit, it won't be hard to find some of the famous Irish wit being dispensed alongside the whiskey and Guinness in Dublin's pubs.

From left to right: Dara O'Briain, Sean Hughes, Jason Byrne

Design & Architecture

At the beginning of the 21st century, during a decade of economic highs, Dublin underwent rapid changes. The traditional image of the city – Guinness, fiddle bands and cosy pubs – came face to face with a bold new world. At the forefront were Dublin's own architects and designers and the biggest makeover was in the Docklands.

Dublin has a highly regarded coterie of designers, many of whom have graduated from the Dublin Institute of Design and the National College of Art and Design. At the peak of the city's boom period, building contracts also attracted some of the biggest names in the world. Today Dublin, like the rest of Ireland, might have come down to earth financially, but the transformations are here to stay. Projects that were years in the planning (and temporarily put on hold) have resumed and spectacular new buildings have emerged.

Docklands Development

Dublin's Docklands spent decades in gradual decline. By 2010, however, its transformation, on both sides of the river, had taken shape. Bridges, towers, theatres and apartments, the Dockland's scheme features a little bit of every- thing – and all can be

The Seán O'Casey Bridge spans the River Liffey

reached by bus or on foot. One of the first projects to be completed was the Seán O'Casey bridge, an elegant footbridge adjacent to the chq Building, an 1821 tobacco warehouse with a cast-iron frame designed by John Rennie that has been transformed into a retail, dining and leisure venue. Go further east and you'll reach the Point Village development, where the Point Theatre has been replaced by the 3Arena music venue with the new Gibson Hotel next door. A shopping centre is also imminent while the new glass-fronted Convention Centre Dublin has already been open for some time. The U2 Tower, set to be the tallest building in Ireland, has been put on hold.

Grand Canal Square

On the south side of the river, building is advanced on some of Dockland's most startling work. Due east from Trinity College is Grand Canal Square, which is being transformed by US architect Martha Schwartz. One of Europe's largest city squares, by day it is an exhilarating public space, by night a dramatically-lit setting for the Grand Canal Theatre, with a forest of glowing red poles creating an exciting visual interpretation of a red carpet. The theatre itself, designed by one of the stars of contemporary architecture, Daniel Libeskind, is an angular, asymmetrical structure of steel and plate glass.

DUBLIN'S MODERN MARVELS

- **The Spire of Dublin** At 120m (394ft), the Spire is the tallest structure in Dublin. The stainless steel landmark was erected in the centre of O'Connell Street in 2003 to replace Nelson's Pillar, which was blown up in 1966.
- **The U2 Tower** On the south side of the Liffey, this will stand at the end of Sir John Rogerson's Quay when it is completed. The 100m (328ft) tower will feature apartments, shops and restaurants and a studio for U2.
- **Grand Canal Square** This vast square provides an illuminated "red carpet" for the theatre and green spaces made from marsh plants. The canal comprises one watery side. It was completed in 2007.
- **Grand Canal Theatre** Daniel Libeskind's masterpiece juts out over Grand Canal Square and looks spectacular at dark.
- **Aviva Stadium** The former Lansdowne Road Stadium is now a 50,000-seater state-of-the-art stadium with a transparent roof. It opened in 2010.

NORTHSIDE VS SOUTHSIDE

The rivalry between the people of north and south Dublin is legendary. Divided by the Liffey, the city has long been split economically and socially, a division exacerbated by the transformation of Temple Bar into a smart cultural quarter. Now, however, times are changing, for the Northside is also undergoing radical redevelopment.

The regeneration of Docklands and the International Financial Centre and the reformation of Smithfield Market have added a new-found vitality to the Northside. Though some of the tenement districts and housing estates further north are on the grim side, and in stark contrast to the leafy Georgian Squares south of the Liffey, regeneration is gradually spreading its tentacles northwards and further west along the river.

The most fashionable address in town is Dublin 4 – Southside, of course – embracing the districts of Ballsbridge, Donnybrook and Sandycove. Leafy Ballsbridge with its elegant Georgian residences is especially exclusive, and popularly known as the Embassy District on account of the large number of foreign embassies located here. Also in Ballsbridge are Lansdowne Road stadium (now Aviva Stadium), the home of the Irish national rugby team, and the Royal Dublin Society Showgrounds, host to the Dublin Horse Show (▶ 27) held in August.

Neighbouring Sandymount is famous for its seaside promenade, which runs all the way to Dun Laoghaire. South of here is Sandycove and the **James Joyce Museum**, housed in the Martello tower that featured in *Ulysses*.

On the Dart
The DART railway is the best way to explore outlying districts of Dublin:

Southbound
- **Dalkey:** This attractive Southside seaside village of brightly painted villas was once called the "Town of Seven Castles", but only two of these fortified mansions remain. Just offshore, Dalkey Island can be visited by boat in summer.
- **Killiney:** This Southside address is home to Formula One driver Damon Hill, U2's Bono and other celebrities. The climb to the top of Killiney Hill is rewarded with sensational coastal vistas.

Northbound
- **Malahide:** This affluent town just north of Dublin looks across the Broadmeadow Estuary. Its most famous sight is Malahide Castle, former family home of the Talbots and open to the public for tours.
- **Howth:** This north Dublin seaside suburb and fishing port is one of the city's most sought-after addresses, bustling with top-notch fish restaurants, lively pubs and a large sailing fraternity. The promontory of Howth Head (▶ 168), overlooking Dublin Bay, is popular with walkers.

Top: Ha'penny Bridge; centre: Smithfield Village; bottom: Dining in Howth

Peace & Quiet

Few people associate Dublin with parks and gardens, yet there are a surprising number of green spaces for recreation and ornamentation within the city centre.

Most people relax in **Phoenix Park** (► 126), one of the world's largest urban parks, with its lush parkland, ancient oak trees, wild deer, memorials and zoo. Others snatch a 10-minute stroll or spend their lunch hour in **Archbishop Ryan Park**, the elegant gardens of Merrion Square (► 111), with its dazzling floral displays and unusual collection of old Dublin lamp-posts; or in **St Stephen's Green** (► 104), a surprisingly serene central park, with ponds, fountains and flowerbeds.

Iveagh Gardens

Insider Tip

Those in the know head to quiet, understated **Iveagh Gardens** (✚ 188 A3), one of the city's finest parks yet surprisingly one of the least well known, situated just a stone's throw from St Stephen's Green (the main entrance is in Clonmel Street). It was originally the private walled grounds of Clonmel House, owned by the Guinness family until 1940. With its maze, grotto, fountains, rose gardens and woodlands, this wild, unkempt park makes you feel you've escaped Dublin altogether.

Secret Gardens

For a quick dose of greenery in the centre, make for the statue-filled little park attached to St Patrick's Cathedral (⊞ 190 B1), or **St Audoen's Park** (⊞ 190 A2), a small park adjoining St Audoen's Protestant church, bounded by the medieval city wall and gates. On the Northside, a 10-minute walk from O'Connell Street, the former reservoir of **Blessington Street Basin** (⊞ 183 F2) is now a quiet haven.

In the northern suburbs, magnificent **St Anne's Park and Rose Gardens** (⊞ off 185 F4) was once part of the home of the Guinness family. It is now a public park, with extensive woodlands, hidden walled gardens, tree-lined walks, an ornamental lake and rose gardens.

Just beyond, **North Bull Island** (⊞ off 185 F4) in Dublin Bay is a nature reserve and bird sanctuary of international importance, with up to 25,000 wading birds here in winter and great beach walks all year round.

Remembrance Gardens

The **War Memorial Gardens** (⊞ 186 B4), on the southern banks of the Liffey facing Phoenix Park, commemorate the 49,000 Irish soldiers who died in World War I. Designed by English architect Sir Edwin Lutyens, they are a must-see for those interested in both gardens and architecture.

The **Garden of Remembrance** (⊞ 184 A2) at the northern end of Parnell Square was opened in 1966 on the 50th anniversary of the Easter Rising (▶ 58) and is dedicated to all those who died for the cause of Irish independence. Ironically, the Easter Rising was plotted in a house nearby and the captured rebels were held prisoner in this square overnight. The large bronze *Children of Lír* sculpture by Oisín Kelly at the far end of the park alludes to ancient Irish myth. It represents the four children of the sea god Lír who were turned into swans by their stepmother, leaving them only their human voice.

Left: Relaxing on the grass. Below: Beside the lake at St Stephen's Green

MUSICAL
DUBLIN

Craic agus Ceol – Music and Fun

Dublin is renowned for its packed pubs alive with the sound of traditional music, but it also has a revered rock 'n' roll heritage, world-class classical concerts and a well established jazz scene.

Traditional Irish Music

For many, the quintessential Irish night out is *craic agus ceol*, music and fun – a pint of Guinness and some live music featuring a fiddle, guitar, tin whistle and *bodhrán* (drum) in a pub. While you'll have to book ahead to see shows like Riverdance and Lord of the Dance, or major artists like Christy Moore or The Chieftains at The Gaiety Theatre (46 King Street South, D2; tel: 0818 719 388; www.gaiety theatre.ie) or 3Arena (North Wall, D1; tel: 0818 719 300; www.3arena. ie), there's no shortage of pubs with live music in Dublin. The best venues include The Brazen Head (20 Bridge Street, D8; tel: 01 677 9549; www.brazenhead.com), Oliver St John Gogarty (58–59 Fleet Street, D2; tel: 01 677 1822; www.gogartys.ie), The Temple Bar (48 Temple Bar, D2; tel: 01 672 5287; www.thetemplebarpub.com) and The Cobblestone (77 North King Street, D7; tel: 01 872 1799; www. cobblestonepub.ie).

Rock and Popular Music

Thin Lizzy, U2 and The Pogues are the mighty moguls of the music scene in Dublin. They set the pace for other up-and-coming groups. The biggest play at 3Arena (see above), but other venues are Vicar Street (58–59 Thomas Street, D8; tel: 01 775 5800; www.vicarstreet.com), Whelans (25 Wexford Street, D2; tel: 01 478 0766; www.whelanslive. com), Olympia Theatre (72 Dame Street, D2; tel: 01 679 3323; www.

Top: Playing the Irish fiddle

Middle: Bono and Adam Clayton from U2

Bottom: Shane MacGowan

olympia.ie), Tripod, Crawdaddy (POD, Old Harcourt Station, Harcourt Street, D2; tel: 01 473 5576) and The Button Factory (Curved Street, D2; tel: 01 670 9202; www.buttonfactory.ie).

For local bands, try The Twisted Pepper (54 Middle Abbey Street, D1; tel: 01 873 40338; www.bodytonicmusic.com), The Porterhouse (16–18 Parliament Street, D2; tel: 01 679 8847; www.the porterhouse.ie) and The Foggy Dew (1 Fownes Street, D2; tel: 01 677 9328; www.the foggydew.ie).

The Gaiety Theatre is one of Dublin's oldest theatres and has seating for 1,100 patrons

Classical Concerts and Opera

Dublin's premier orchestra is the RTÉ Symphony Orchestra, and you might be able to book tickets to hear it play at the National Concert Hall (NCH) (2 Earlsfort Terrace, D2; tel: 01 417 0000; www.nch.ie). The RTÉ Concert Orchestra, Vanbrugh Quartet, RTÉ Philharmonic Choir and the RTÉ Cór na nÓg (Youth Choir) are all part of the same group and also perform regularly at the NCH. Ireland's National Opera Company, Opera Ireland, presents a couple of operas each season at The Gaiety Theatre (►36) as well as lunchtime arias, which you can enjoy over a bite to eat in the theatre's Dress Circle Bar.

Jazz and Blues

The veteran jazz and blues bar is JJ Smyths (12 Aungier Street, D2; tel: 01 475 2565; www.jjsmyths.com), which offers a packed programme of concerts most nights of the week. The Boom Boom Room (Patrick Conways Pub, 70 Parnell Street, D1; tel: 01 873 2687; www.boomboom room.weebly.com) is the new hip kid on the block, where the music is offbeat and underground. Other venues where you might find jazz, blues or Cajun, bluegrass and global sounds, include The Globe (11 South Great George's Street, D2; tel: 01 671 1220; www.theglobe.ie) and the Voodoo Lounge (39–40 Arran Quay, D7; tel: 01 873 6013).

Finding Your Feet

First Two Hours

Dublin is well served by its international airport, two ferry ports and two railway stations. Both ports and the airport have foreign exchange bureaux, branches of the major car-rental firms, bus transfers to the city centre and taxi ranks.

Arriving By Air

- Dublin Airport is **12km (7.5mi) north of the city centre**. In 2010 a second terminal opened to handle Aer Lingus flights and other long-haul operators.
- **To get to Dublin city centre by car**, take the M1 south and follow signs. The journey takes between 20 minutes and an hwour depending on the volume of traffic.
- **Taxis** are metered and a journey to the centre should be €20–30. The taxi rank is on the Arrivals level. Be prepared to wait.
- To get to **Dublin city centre by bus**, there are several options. Airlink bus No 747 leaves every 15 minutes from Arrivals to O'Connell Street, Busáras (the central bus terminal) and Parnell Square. Airlink bus No 748 will also take you to Tara Street, Aston Quay and Heuston Station. For further information contact Dublin Bus (tel: 01 873 4222; www.dublinbus.ie). Tickets are available at the CIE Information Desk in Arrivals.
- If you plan to use the bus regularly in the city centre, consider buying one of the special **Rambler bus passes** (➤ 41).
- The **Aircoach express service** operates 24 hours a day from Arrivals every 10 minutes at peak times. City-centre stops include O'Connell Street, Grafton Street, Merrion Square North, Pembroke Road and St Stephen's Green. Tickets are available from the Tourist Information desk in Arrivals. For information contact Aircoach (tel: 01 844 7118; www.aircoach.ie).
- The **cheapest way into the city** is by public bus (Nos 16A, 41, 41A, 41B and 41C); buses operate every 10–20 minutes from the airport to Eden Quay, near O'Connell Street. These are slower than the Airlink and Aircoach services, with numerous stops *en route*.

Arriving By Boat

- **Ferries from the UK** sail into either Dublin Port, 5km (3mi) east of Dublin city centre, or Dun Laoghaire ("Dunleary"), 14km (9mi) south of the city.
- If **travelling by car** from the ports to Dublin, simply follow city-centre signs.
- **Taxis and coaches** operate from both ports into the centre of Dublin.
- **Public buses** run regularly to the centre: catch Nos 7, 7A or 46A from Dun Laoghaire DART Station; Nos 53 or 53A from Dublin Port. A special Dublin Bus shuttles between the ferry terminal and Busáras (the central bus station) every half-hour 7am–11:10pm daily. The journey takes around 10 minutes.
- **An inexpensive DART service** (➤ 40) from Dun Laoghaire to Dublin runs every half-hour (sometimes more frequently) to Pearse, Tara Street and Connolly stations in the city centre. The journey takes 25 minutes.

Arriving By Train

- Dublin has **two mainline stations**. Passengers from the north arrive at Connolly Station, while trains from the south and west operate in and out of Heuston Station. Buses and taxis are available at both stations.
- For **rail information**, contact Irish Rail/Iarnród Éireann (tel: reservations 01 836 6222; Mon–Fri 8:30–6 only; www.irishrail.ie).

Tourist Information Offices

- The **main Dublin tourist office** is located inside a converted church in Suffolk Street. It can help make reservations and supply information on what's on.
- **Dublin Tourism**, 25 Suffolk Street, D2 (www.visitdublin.com; open Jul–Aug Mon–Sat 9–7, Sun 10:30–3; Sep–Jun Mon–Sat 9–5:30, Sun 10:30–3).
- Several other tourist information offices are placed at strategic spots around the city: **Dun Laoghaire Ferry Terminal** (Mon–Fri 9:30–1:15, 2:30–5:30); **Dublin Airport Arrivals Hall** (daily 8am–10pm); **17 O'Connell Street** (Mon–Sat 9–5).
- The website of the **Irish Tourist Board** (www.discoverireland.ie) is useful for information on Ireland in general.
- The **Dublin Pass** gives free entry to 32 attractions and other offers, including transport to and from Dublin airport. It is available as a 1-, 2-, 3- or 6-day pass.
- The **Leap Visitor Card** is valid for Dublin Bus, the Airlink airport bus service, Bus Éireann services in the surrounding counties, the LUAS tramway services and the DART in the Short Hop Zone. It is available as a 1-day (€10), 3-day (€19.50) or 7-day (€40) pass and can be purchased at the airport and in Spar shops (www.leapcard.ie).

Getting Around

Dublin is divided into two halves by the River Liffey, which neatly bisects the city from east to west. These two areas are popularly referred to as Northside and Southside.

Public Transport

Buses are the main form of public transport in the city, with the DART (Dublin Area Rapid Transit) train system and the LUAS tramway being the most popular ways to reach the suburbs. (►transport map on the inside back cover for all routes.)

Bus

- **Dublin Bus** operates a **comprehensive network** of bus routes throughout the city and into the suburbs, Mon–Sat 6am–11:30pm, Sun 10am–11:30pm, and a **Nitelink limited** service on selected routes Mon–Sat after midnight. For route details, contact Dublin Bus (tel: 01 873 4222; www.dublinbus.ie).
- The **number** and **destination** (in English and Irish) are displayed on the front of each bus. *An Lar* means city centre.
- **Tickets** can be bought on the bus (no change given). **Timetables** and **pre-paid tickets** can be bought from the Dublin Bus desk at the airport, the main ticket office (59 O'Connell Street Upper, D1; open Mon–Fri 9–5:30, Sat 9–2) or at any of the 300 Dublin Bus ticket agents around the city.
- The 1-, 3- or 5-day **Rambler Ticket** offers unlimited travel for consecutive days on all Dublin Bus scheduled services, including the Airlink bus service (►40), excluding Nitelink and special tours.
- The **Dublin Freedom Pass** is valid for three days and includes airport transfers with Airlink, the green hop-on hop-off sightseeing bus and all buses in Dublin (3 days €33; www.dublinsightseeing.ie; tickets available at the airport, in tourist offices and at the Airlink counter).

Finding Your Feet

- If you plan to explore County Dublin, consider an **Adult Short Hop pass**, valid for unlimited travel for one day for one adult on all Dublin Bus, DART and Suburban Rail scheduled services; a **Family Short Hop day pass** valid for immediate family members (not exceeding two adults and four children under 16 years).
- Special **student passes** are available on production of a current ISIC Card.
- All tickets must be inserted into the **ticket validator** as you enter the bus.

DART

- The **DART** (Dublin Area Rapid Transit) is a **light rail service**, operated by Irish Rail, serving 31 stations from Malahide in the north to Greystones in the south.
- Main city-centre stations are **Connolly** (north of the river), and **Tara Street** and **Pearse** (both south of the river).
- **Trains run** every five minutes in rush hours, every 10–15 minutes at other times of the day Mon–Sat 6:30am–midnight and less frequently Sun 9:30am–11pm.
- **Single tickets** are available from any DART station, but it can be cheaper to buy a one-day unlimited DART travel ticket or a family pass. Validating machines, where provided, must be used.
- Irish Rail sells **a range of combined travel passes** in conjunction with Dublin Bus (➤ 41) and the LUAS tramway.

LUAS

- A new **tramway** system opened in 2004. At present it has only two routes (organized into seven zones) to the suburbs, primarily used by commuters.
- LUAS offers a range of ticket options from a single trip to a 30-day pass, together with 1-, 7- and 30-day **Combi-tickets** for LUAS and Dublin Bus.

Taxi

- There are **plenty of taxis** in Dublin, but on Friday and Saturday nights you may have to wait for a short while.
- Taxis are found at **taxi ranks** or can be **hailed on the street**.

Driving

- Traffic in Ireland **drives on the left**.
- Drivers and all passengers must wear **seat belts**.
- **The speed limit** is 50kph (31mph) in towns, 80kph (50mph) on regional roads, 100kph (62 mph) on national roads and dual carriageways, and 120kph (74mph) on motorways.
- The **legal alcohol limit** is 80mg alcohol per 100ml blood (8 per cent) (tel: 01 499 9601).
- The volume of traffic is increasing and **parking is expensive** and limited.
- Try to avoid weekday morning and late-afternoon rush hours (7:30–8/9am and 4–6), keep out of bus lanes and use car parks.
- The **North and South Circular roads** circumscribe the core of Dublin, and most of the city's sights are located within this area. The city's main thoroughfare is **O'Connell Street**. The quays alongside the Liffey are one-way: the south bank flows east to west and the north bank west to east.
- **Traffic wardens** take their job seriously and tow-away trucks are plentiful.
- The **M50** motorway, a ring road around Dublin, is a **toll road**. Cars cost €3.10 and the toll must be paid by 8pm on the day following the journey. You can pay online at www.eflow.ie, by telephone using a credit card at LoCall 1 890 501 050 and at Payzone branded petrol station and shops,

such as Spar. Failure to pay the toll will result in the following charges: one day late €3, the next 14 days €41 and after a further 56 days €102.50. Your car rental company will charge unpaid tolls and fines to your credit card.

Car Rental

■ All the main **car-rental companies** have desks in the Arrivals Hall at Dublin airport and in the city centre. Contact **Hertz** (tel: 01 844 5466), **Budget** (tel: 01 844 5150), **Avis** (tel: 01 605 7566), **Sixt** (tel: 01 844 5691), **Europcar** (tel: 01 812 2800).

■ **Dooley Car Rental** has a desk at **Dun Laoghaire Harbour** (tel: 01 842 8864).

Postal Codes

Dublin is divided into 24 postal codes with unevenly numbered districts north of the Liffey and even ones to the south. The central areas, where the main sights are located, are D1 and D2.

D1 the main hub of the north bank.

D2 the heart of the south bank, including the main shopping district, Temple Bar, Trinity College and many of the key city sights.

D4 south and southeast of D2; this is one of Dublin's smartest districts, boasting some of its finest Georgian architecture.

D7 the western end of Northside, including Smithfield and Phoenix Park.

D8 the western end of Southside, including much of Viking and medieval Dublin, the two cathedrals and the Guinness factory.

In 2015 Ireland introduced a seven-digit postal code, the Eircode system, and now each house has its own address code.

Accommodation

Dublin is divided economically as well as geographically by the River Liffey, with the north inner-city tending to provide cheaper accommodation than the south side.

■ The most **exclusive hotels**, including the Merrion, the Shelbourne, the Clarence and the Fitzwilliam, offer top-notch world-class facilities with prices to match. These are all well located in the heart of town.

■ You will also find many attractive **Georgian town houses**, which have been converted into small hotels and guest-houses, offering modern comforts in graceful surroundings while at the same time providing a glimpse of Dublin's glorious past.

■ **Further out**, the tariffs will be lower and the buildings more recent (probably Victorian or Edwardian), but be prepared for a short bus or taxi ride into the city centre.

■ If you have a **car**, think about staying even further out in the more peaceful suburbs, or on the coast at Portmarnock (➤ 46).

■ If you are on a **tight budget** and want to **stay centrally**, consider a hostel. You may have to share facilities, but an increasing number have private rooms. Among the best are **Isaacs** (2–5 Frenchmans Lane, D1; tel: 01 855 6215; www.isaacs.ie), one of the longest-established, best-known hostels, in a converted wine warehouse north of the river, near the central bus station; **Ashfield House** (19 D'Olier Street, D2; tel: 01 679 7734; www. ashfieldhouse.ie), once a church, now with clean, spacious twin rooms;

Finding Your Feet

and **Barnacles** (19 Temple Lane, D2; tel: 01 671 6277; www.barnacles.ie), hugely popular and situated right at the heart of trendy Temple Bar.

Booking Accommodation

- You'll find competitive last-minute deals, but during holiday periods and major sports fixtures it's best to **book well ahead**.
- Rates quoted below include service charges and VAT. Prices can double during peak periods; some hotels offer reduced rates for quieter periods.
- Go Ireland offers an **on-the-spot booking service** for hotels, hostels, B&Bs, guest-houses and self-catering premises for Dublin Tourism and other tourist information offices.
- Reservations can be made **on-line** through the Irish Tourist Board website (www.discoverireland.ie) and Dublin Tourism (www.visitdublin.com).

Accommodation Prices
Prices are for two people sharing a double room per night

€ under €100   €€ €100–€200   €€€ over €200

Aberdeen Lodge €€

This charming private hotel in an elegant, restored Edwardian house combines century-old style with modern comforts, friendly service, a large garden and great food – including award-winning breakfasts. Set in an attractive tree-lined avenue in the quiet residential Southside suburb of Ballsbridge (► 32), close to the car ferry terminals and just five minutes' walk from the Sydney Parade DART Station, it makes a perfect base for exploring both the city centre and the Wicklow Mountains.

Insider Tip

➕ 189 E2 ✉ 53 Park Avenue, D4
☎ 01 283 8155; www.aberdeen-lodge.com

Butlers Town House Hotel €€

This beautifully presented Victorian town house offers 20 rooms combining period features and luxurious furnishings with modern comforts, including power showers, four-poster beds and 24-hour room service. There is a cosy drawing room where guests can enjoy a nightcap, and gourmet breakfasts are served in the conservatory restaurant. It's situated a stone's throw from the new Aviva Stadium and has on-site parking.

➕ 188 C3 ✉ 44 Lansdowne Road, D4
☎ 01 667 4022; www.butlers-townhouse.ie

Clarence €€€

This swish, minimalist, boutique hotel in Temple Bar is the trendiest address in town – a converted 19th-century Customs House on the banks of the Liffey owned by U2 band members Bono and The Edge. It offers all the luxuries and amenities expected by the many celebrities who stay here, with astonishing attention to detail. Treat yourself to a night in the multi-level penthouse suite. Costing from €1,090 per night, with an outdoor hot tub overlooking the river, this is surely Dublin's ultimate extravagance.

➕ 190 C3 ✉ 6–8 Wellington Quay, D2
☎ 01 407 0800; www.theclarence.ie

The Spencer IFSC €€–€€€

Built with the business visitor in mind – it's right in the centre of the International Financial Services Centre – this high-rise, modern hotel has been a surprising hit with tourists. The rooms are big, bright and cheery and ideal for families. Ask for one at the front so you can enjoy the great views over the mouth of the Liffey. Because it caters mostly to business travellers weekend bargains are often on offer.

➕ 192 C4 ✉ Excise Walk, IFSC, D1
☎ 01 433 8800; www.thespencerhotel.com

Dylan €€€

A recent addition to Dublin's 5-star hotels, Dylan exudes fashion-conscious style in each of its 44 bespoke guest rooms as well as in its restaurant and bar. Expect low French-style beds and flashes of colour on feature walls and textiles, lit by contemporary chandeliers. There are also lots of hi-tech gadgets, including Tilevision TVs in some bathrooms.

⊞ 188 C3 ⊠ East Moreland Place, D4
☎ 01 660 3000; www.dylan.ie

Fitzwilliam €€–€€€

You couldn't wish for a finer or more central location than this. Near Grafton Street (➤ 109) and overlooking St Stephen's Green (➤ 104), this hotel oozes modern comforts, impeccable service and understated luxury. Its interiors, created by English designer Terence Conran, are inspired by a design concept entitled "Baronial Modern" – a modern interpretation of a country house, with frosted glass, leather sofas, angular surfaces, moody down-lighting and accents of cream, purple and chrome. Top-floor front rooms have balconies with views of the Green; others overlook the country's largest roof garden. One of Ireland's top chefs, Kevin Thornton, has his highly acclaimed eponymous restaurant here (➤ 117).

⊞ 191 E1 ⊠ St Stephen's Green, D2
☎ 01 478 7000; www.fitzwilliamhoteldublin.com

Grand Canal Hotel €–€€

On the far side of the canal from the new developments around Grand Canal Square, this modern hotel is close enough to benefit from the cultural amenities. The restaurant, bar and coffee shop are characterless but the rooms are clean and contemporary, there is safe parking, a new gym, and a DART station across the road.

⊞ 188 C4 ⊠ Grand Canal Street Upper, Ballsbridge, D4 ☎ 01 646 1000; www.grandcanalhotel.ie

Harding €–€€

This bright, cheerful and stylish hotel proves you can be comfortable on a budget. Most of the 52 rooms sleep three people and all have private bathrooms. At the heart of historic Dublin (the city's oldest street, Copper Alley, runs through the reception area), it is conveniently close to many of the main sights.

⊞ 190 C3 ⊠ Copper Alley, Fishamble Street, D2
☎ 01 679 6500; www.hardinghotel.ie

Hilton Kilmainham €€

Located opposite Kilmainham Gaol and IMMA, where the tour buses stop, and a 15-minute walk from Heuston Station, this modern hotel is a good alternative to hotels located in the bustling city centre. The rooms are quiet, spacious and contemporary, and the breakfasts ample. Excellent communal facilities include a gym, spa, restaurant and parking.

⊞ 186 B4 ⊠ Inchicore Road, D8 ☎ 01 420 1800; www.hilton.co.uk/dublinkilmainham

Merrion €€€

Dublin's most luxurious five-star hotel consists of four Georgian town houses, sensitively restored to combine period elegance with top-class modern facilities. The 18th-century-style landscaped gardens help to create a peaceful retreat. The hotel is connected to the eponymous restaurant of the celebrated Irish chef Patrick Guilbaud (➤ 116).

⊞ 192 B1 ⊠ Merrion Street Upper, D2
☎ 01 603 0600; www.merrionhotel.com

Mont Clare €€

This is a large, friendly hotel with an attractive Georgian facade and well-equipped rooms offering excellent value for money, in a fantastic location just around the corner from Trinity College, the National Gallery and the main shopping areas. There is also a traditional pub on the ground floor.

⊞ 192 C2 ⊠ 1–4 Merrion Street Lower, D2
☎ 01 607 3800; www.montclarehotel.ie

Finding Your Feet

Morgan Hotel €€

Hidden amid the boutiques and pubs of the vibrant Temple Bar area, this boutique hotel offers luxury city-centre accommodation at an affordable price. The 61 rooms are minimalist and chic, with internet access and great emphasis on aesthetic detail. For more space or to hold your own private party, the Penthouse has its own baby grand piano and access to a rooftop garden with its own retro Airstream caravan. Downstairs in the Morgan Bar you can enjoy a coffee, or cocktails and tapas, in the courtyard.

✚ 191 E3 ✉ 10 Fleet Street, Temple Bar, D02AT86 ☎ 01 643 7097; www.themorgan.com

Morrison €€–€€€

Superbly located on the north bank of the Liffey, the Morrison is a marvel of modern design. When the hotel was established, Ireland's top designer, John Rocha, had the last word on everything from toilets to staff uniforms. It is smart, modern and sumptuous – a minimalist juxtaposition of wood, stone, steel and velvet – providing an exotic, serene haven far removed from the madness of the city centre on the doorstep. Its esteemed Halo restaurant (➤ 140) has been restyled to retain its fashionable ambience and clientele.

✚ 190 C3 ✉ Ormond Quay Lower, D1 ☎ 01 887 2400; www.morrisonhotel.ie

Number 31 €€

This award-winning B&B in the heart of Georgian Dublin is just a few minutes' walk from St Stephen's Green. The former home of Sam Stephenson, Ireland's leading architect, it offers a choice of 21 stylish rooms, with many luxurious touches, spread over two striking buildings – a coach-house and a handsome town house – overlooking Fitzwilliam Place. Guests are very much encouraged to make themselves at home.

✚ 188 B3 ✉ 31 Leeson Close, D2 ☎ 01 676 5011; www.number31.ie

The Schoolhouse Hotel €€

This intimate and unusual hotel, housed in a former schoolhouse in trendy Ballsbridge, exudes a warm, friendly atmosphere. The superbly appointed bedrooms combine old-world charm with modern conveniences. It has retained many original features from its days as a school, and its former classrooms now house The Canteen restaurant and the lively Schoolhouse bar. It is gaining a reputation for quality modern Irish cuisine in an unusual setting.

✚ 188 C4 ✉ 2–3 Northumberland Road, D4 ☎ 01 667 5014; www.schoolhousehotel.com

The Shelbourne Hotel €€€

The renovated Shelbourne (➤ 116) has been rated Dublin's most distinguished hotel, and it has hosted royal and famous guests ever since its opening in the 18th century. Authors as diverse as Thackeray and Elizabeth Bowen have sung its praises in their work. In 1921, it was the setting for the signing of the Irish constitution. Today, with its luxurious rooms, two bars, two restaurants, spa and health centre, it ranks among the greatest hotels of the world – opulent and extravagant, yet surprisingly personal. A wonderful place for afternoon tea.

✚ 191 F1 ✉ 27 St Stephen's Green, D2 ☎ 01 663 4500; www.marriott.com

FURTHER AFIELD

Portmarnock Hotel and Golf Links €€–€€€

This luxurious seaside hotel is the former home of the Jameson whiskey family. It has an award-winning restaurant, spa and an 18-hole golf course designed by Bernhard Langer. Located a 20-minute drive from the city centre, it is ideally placed for visiting Malahide (➤ 151), Howth (➤ 168) and north County Dublin, and makes a relaxing alternative to a city-centre hotel.

✚ 185 off F5 ✉ Portmarnock, County Dublin ☎ 01 846 0611; www.portmarnock.com

Food and Drink

Eating out in Dublin has never been better. Restaurants and pubs have been opening with bewildering speed in the city over the past few years. A host of talented, young Irish chefs have appeared on the scene, and there is a noticeable emphasis on good-quality local ingredients. What's more, there is an abundance of choice.

Many of the most favoured eateries can be found around Temple Bar and in the busy network of streets between Dawson Street and South Great George's Street, but some of the real culinary gems lie further afield in the lesser-known back streets and suburbs. Whether you're after a gourmet feast, a stylish meal somewhere chic, a cheap-and-cheerful snack, or wholesome, hearty pub food, one thing's for sure – eating out in Dublin combines hospitality, high standards of cooking, choice ingredients and good value for money.

Restaurant Prices
Expect to pay for a three-course meal, excluding drinks but including VAT
€ under €30   €€ €30–€50   €€€ over €50

International Cooking

■ Changes in **food fashions** have resulted in dramatic developments on the restaurant front recently, with the emergence of numerous minimalist *nouveau* eateries with strong emphasis on **global cuisine**. Mediterranean, Tex-Mex, Asian fusion, Indian, Italian…all the main cuisines are well represented in the city, with Thai and Japanese restaurants making a particular impact. This diversity is relatively new to Ireland and is something which local chefs have seized upon with great enthusiasm. As a result, many of these restaurants offer an astonishing range of ingredients and flavours, combined in innovative ways.

Irish Cooking

■ Alongside foreign cuisine, Irish cooking has made a comeback. The city's top chefs are working on the concept of a **Modern Irish Cuisine** – light, modern interpretations of traditional dishes and ingredients (➤ 25).

■ At the other end of the scale, simple and nourishing **traditional Irish fare** (➤ 24) remains the order of the day in some restaurants, although it is usually easier to find in pubs.

Pubs

■ Dublin's pubs used to exist for **drinking not dining**, but these days most pubs offer excellent food at lunchtime and some offer meals into the early evening too. For many visitors, the **pub atmosphere** is especially enjoyable, allowing them to savour a glass of Guinness or any of the other excellent Irish-brewed beers with their meal. Many pubs will serve coffee at any time of day, including **Irish coffee** – a delicious concoction of coffee, cream and whiskey, which is perfect on a cold day.

■ For decades, all the **city pubs** were very similar – smoky, intimate and full of locals. Then, as Dublin began to flourish, glitzy, new-wave,

Finding Your Feet

lounge-style bars, trendy mega-pubs and theme bars (which locals disparagingly call "Euro-swiggers") began to open, drawing a young crowd, and pandering to the stag- and hen-night celebrants on weekends.

- Along with the city's great icon drink of *Guinness*, some pubs are now serving **new stouts and ales** made by Ireland's new micro-breweries, such as The Porterhouse (➤ 86).
- Even though Dublin has changed considerably in recent years, the pub remains at the very **hub of the city's social life**, and with more than a thousand pubs listed in the Dublin phone book, you will find watering-holes to suit all tastes.

Cafes

- Like many cities, Dublin has gone crazy over **coffee**. Apart from the well-known international coffee chains, new names such as Insomnia and The Bald Barista have sprung up throughout the city alongside old favourites such as Butler's Chocolate Café (➤ 80) and the Avoca Café (➤ 113).
- Cafes are a popular choice for **lunch**, with many of the most attractive cafes located in museums or shopping centres – such as Dublin City Gallery The Hugh Lane (➤ 134), Chester Beatty Library (➤ 73), Dublin Writers Museum (➤ 134) and the Powerscourt Townhouse (➤ 77).

Practical Tips

- **Booking** is essential for many restaurants, particularly at weekends and from spring through to autumn.
- **Lunch is usually served** between 12 and 2:30, dinner between 6 and 11.
- Some of the top restaurants offer **excellent value fixed-price** lunch menus, making elegant dining surprisingly affordable. Many restaurants also have "early bird" deals, usually served around 6–7:30pm.
- **Most pubs open** Mon–Thu 10am–11:30pm, Fri–Sat 10am–12:30am, Sun noon–11pm. Also on Sunday, a few of the more traditional pubs observe "holy hour" and close their doors from 2–4, although if you are already inside you can usually stay and continue to drink.
- Many of the large pubs and music venues, generally described as **"late bars"**, have extended licences at the weekend and will serve customers until 2am.
- A **service charge** of 12.5 per cent is generally added to the bill for parties of six or more in restaurants. When service charge hasn't been added, a tip of 10–15 per cent is the norm.
- **Smoking is banned** in all public places (bars, restaurants, offices, etc).
- **Dress code** is generally relaxed; very few restaurants insist on jacket and tie for men.
- **Menus** are written in English.

Best Traditional Irish Cuisine
- Winding Stair (➤ 141)
- Ely (➤ 114)
- Gallagher's Boxty House (➤ 81)

Best International Cuisine
- L'Gueuleton (➤ 115)
- Chez Max (➤ 80)
- Patrick Guilbaud (➤ 116)

Best Coffee and Cakes
- Avoca Café (➤ 113)
- The Queen of Tarts (➤ 72)

Best for Beer
- Mulligan's (➤ 119)
- Grogan's (➤ 85)
- The Porterhouse (➤ 86)
- The Gravediggers (➤ 143)

Shopping

Dublin's image as a city of souvenir shops stuffed with lucky leprechauns and Celtic kitsch faded and talented home-grown designers and craftsmen sprang up to give the country's traditional elements of wood, silver, linen and wool new forms. But what really sets Dublin apart from many other major cities is the wonderful mix of independent shops.

- The bustling **city centre** provides the ideal setting for shopping, with some 3,000 shops and boutiques, many of which are still family owned.
- It's easy to walk around the main shopping areas in a day without the need for public transport and the creation of pedestrian zones in two areas of the city has made shopping a particularly enjoyable experience: the **two main thoroughfares** – Henry Street (on the north side) with its high-street chain stores and good-value department shops, and Grafton Street (on the south side) with its chic boutiques.
- The maze of streets around **Grafton Street** contains an intriguing mix of ultra-hip boutiques, old-fashioned stores and tiny off-beat shops making shopping here a delight. *Insider Tip*
- **Temple Bar** is a popular area for souvenirs, off-centre kitsch and trendy urban wear.
- The abundant **local specialities and crafts** make unique souvenirs. They range from delicate handmade jewellery, based on ancient Celtic designs, to hand-thrown ceramics and traditional musical instruments, while food and drink will keep the distinctive tastes of Dublin fresh long after your return home.

Antiques and Art

- **Antiques** can still be a good buy in Dublin, especially Georgian Irish furniture and silver (look for the harp in the hallmark), and early 20th-century Irish art has attracted worldwide acclaim.
- There are many commercial **art galleries** around the city. You can find reviews of exhibitions in *TimeOut Dublin* (www.timeoutdublin.com). The annual Fringe Festival (www.fringefest.com) also sees lots of visual arts coming to town.
- The **main shopping area** for antiques in the city is around Francis Street (► 83), and it's worth checking out the newspapers for local **auctions** too.

Books

Book-lovers will find that the literary capital of Europe won't disappoint. It is easy to while away an afternoon browsing in the the the bookshop at the **Dublin Writers Museum** (► 130), or in one of the city's countless other bookstores.

Fashion

There's no denying it, Dublin is chic! There are dozens of shops to appeal to all tastes and budgets from funky fashion outlets to large department stores, and the city has always had a great choice of antique, retro and second-hand clothing boutiques.

- As well as an abundance of foreign designer labels, local young designers have taken the **international fashion arena** by storm. Names to look out for include Lainey Keogh (knitwear), Louise Kennedy (suits), Philip Treacy (hats), Vivienne Walsh (jewellery), Orla Kiely and Pauric Sweeney

Finding Your Feet

(handbags), together with Quinn & Donnelly (womenswear), MoMuse Jewellery, Heather Finn (knitwear) and Matt Doody (womenswear).

■ You'll find **their work showcased** at the Kilkenny Shop (➤ 117), Brown Thomas (➤ 117), and the Design Centre (➤ 82).

Food & Drink

■ **Traditional Irish foods** that travel well include smoked salmon (buy it vacuum packed); some of the firmer farmhouse cheeses such as Gubbeen and Durrus are also a good buy. They are widely available in delicatessens, specialist cheese shops and supermarkets such as Fallon & Byrne (➤ 84).

■ The Irish are **famous for their drink**, so why not treat yourself to a bottle of Jameson, Powers or one of the numerous other Irish whiskeys that are widely available? Then there's Baileys (one of the world's top-selling drinks), Irish Mist (a sweet liqueur made from whiskey and honey) and Guinness, of course.

Glassware

■ Irish **cut lead crystal** has been produced since the 18th century and is famous throughout the world. The best known is Waterford crystal, which, although mainly made overseas these days, is widely available in department stores and gift shops across the city.

■ Look out for pieces by Irish designer **John Rocha**, who has been defining Irish fashions for more than a decade, and has now, along with Jasper Conran and Michael Arram, brought Waterford crystal back into vogue with clean-cut, minimalist designs.

Handicrafts

■ The shops along Nassau Street (➤ 117) sell some of Ireland's finest **handicrafts**. Look out for timeless tweeds, woollens, linen and lace, as well as delicate hand-cut jewellery, functional and arty ceramics and attractive wrought ironware.

■ **Knitwear** is highly popular and ranges from chunky Aran fishermen's sweaters to sophisticated fashion items made by Lainey Keogh or Heather Finn (above), while **Irish linen** is world famous and hard-wearing – best buys include classic table- and bed-linen.

Music

■ Dublin has an unusually large number of vintage **record shops**.

■ There are also several specialist **traditional and folk music outlets** selling instruments as well as CDs and cassettes.

Practical Tips

■ **Opening hours** for most shops are Monday to Saturday, from 9 or 9:30am until 5:30 or 6pm. Some shops don't open until 10am; some close for lunch; others open on Sundays.

■ Many **city-centre bookshops** keep longer hours, and some also open on Sunday afternoons.

■ Thursday is **late-night shopping**, with the bigger stores and many of the smaller ones remaining open until about 8pm. Supermarkets tend to open late on Fridays.

■ **Payment** can be made in euros (€) or by debit/credit cards.

■ Most high-street shops will **refund or exchange** goods as long as you keep your receipt and return the purchase within 10 days.

Entertainment

Many people come to Dublin simply to have a good time, and they rarely leave disappointed – it's not known as the European party capital for nothing. Going out in Dublin is a way of life. There's singing and dancing, clubs and drink. From cosy, old-fashioned watering-holes to smart designer bars and raucous theme pubs; from theatre to stand-up comedy; from traditional music to jazz; from classical to rock 'n' roll...there's something for everyone here.

Pubs

- The quintessential **Dublin pub** (and there are more than a thousand different pubs to choose from) provides the focal point of many Dubliners' social life. It is here that conversation and *craic* (➤ 36) flows freely, creating an atmosphere that is the essence of Dublin and its friendly inhabitants.
- Many pubs, including O'Donoghue's (➤ 119), The Cobblestone Bar (➤ 144), the Brazen Head (➤ 86) and O'Shea's Merchant (➤ 159), offer live **traditional Irish music**.

Live Music

- **Music and song**, classical, traditional and contemporary, play a large part in most social occasions, often experienced with its natural accompainment – dance.
- The city provides a showcase for a wide variety of musical tastes with numerous **live music venues**. Over the years these have famously given rise to such internationally renowned Irish folk musicians as The Dubliners as well as major rock and pop artists such as U2, Chris de Burgh, Boyzone and The Corrs.
- The most popular **late-night live music** venues for experiencing modern Irish and visiting international acts include Whelans (➤ 85) and The Button Factory (➤ 85).

Clubs

- Dublin is at the **cutting edge** of pub and club culture, probably because of its youthful population. With 30% of all Dubliners under 25, it is the youngest capital city in Europe.
- The most vibrant symbol of Dublin's nightlife is **Temple Bar** (➤ 68). An up-tempo enclave of restaurants and bars with a decidedly raucous atmosphere, it draws a young and often rowdy crowd to its many clubs late at night.
- **Admission charges** vary; some are free. All clubs are pretty busy, especially at weekends.
- **Key city clubs** include Club M and Rí-Rá, both on Southside (➤ 85).

Theatre, Dance, Concerts and Cinema

- Dublin offers a **wonderful array** of dance, theatre, and classical and jazz concerts, from world-class ballet at the National Concert Hall (➤ 120) and Riverdance at The Gaiety (➤ 120) to jovial local street musicians performing on Grafton Street and around Temple Bar.
- The city's long-established **theatre scene** continues to thrive with dozens of mainstream and fringe theatre companies performing at such prestigious venues as the Abbey Theatre (➤ 144), the new Bord Gáis Energy Theatre (➤ 120) and the Gate (➤ 144).

Finding Your Feet

- Popular **Dublin-based dance troupes** include CoisCéim Dance Theatre and the Irish Modern Dance Theatre. Contact www.coisceim.com and www.irishmoderndancetheatre.com.
- Opera Ireland and the Opera Theatre Company perform regularly at a variety of city venues.
- **Comedy and cabaret** also feature strongly, staged at many pubs across the city including The International (➤ 164) on Wednesday nights, and the Ha'Penny Bridge Inn (42 Wellington Quay, D2), on Tuesday and Thursday nights.
- There are numerous multiplex **cinemas** and small cinemas throughout the city centre and suburbs. The Savoy on O'Connell Street and the little Screen cinema beside Trinity College are two old favourites; both have several screens.
- For theatre, concert and cinema details, look in a **listings magazine** (below) or consult the local newspapers.

What's On When?

- Most **daily papers** include detailed listings of theatre, cinema, live music, sporting events and festivals. *The Irish Times* website (www.irishtimes.com) is also a valuable source of information.
- The free listings magazine *In Dublin* (published every two weeks) is distributed in bars, hotels and attractions; it contains information on theatre, cinema, museums, current exhibitions, live music venues, nightclubs and restaurants, as well as the city's thriving gay scene (www.indublin.ie).
- The free *Event Guide* can be found in pubs, cafes, restaurants and record shops and provides a useful source of up-to-date information on all aspects of Dublin's nightlife, together with key events taking place throughout Ireland (www.eventguide.ie).
- *Hot Press* magazine is the bible of music and youth culture in Ireland, and contains comprehensive listings on Dublin's contemporary music and nightlife scene (www.hotpress.com).

Tickets

- Tickets for many events can be obtained on the night, but it is recommended that you **book in advance**, especially for big-name artists, major sporting events and such celebrated shows as Riverdance (www.hotpress.com).

Sport

The Irish are passionate about all kinds of sport, and Dubliners are no exception, so there is much to occupy the sports spectator here, including the very best in Gaelic football, hurling, international rugby, football and horse-racing.

- For keen **golfers**, there are more than a hundred golf courses within a 50km (30mi) radius of Dublin, including the celebrated fairways of the Royal Dublin, Bernhard Langer's Portmarnock Links, Druids Glen and The K Club, the venue of the 2005 Ryder Cup. They all welcome visiting players. Contact Golfnet (tel: 01 505 4000; www.golfnet.ie) for further information.
- **Hiking** is increasingly popular, with a mass exodus of Dubliners at weekends to the coast at Howth (➤ 168) and Bray Head, and to the Wicklow Mountains (➤ 148).
- The 136km (85mi) **Wicklow Way**, one of Ireland's longest waymarked paths, starts in a southern suburb of Rathfarnham.

Southside West

 Little Treats

A Fisherman's Heaven
You can marvel at the virtually inexhaustible range of fishing and tackle equipment in **Rory's Fishing Tackle** (➤ 68) at 17A Temple Bar.

Want to Mingle with Celebrities?
Then head for the **Octagon Bar** (➤ 84) in the Clarence Hotel. Owned by Bono and The Edge it is popular with Irish actors and musicians.

Take a Break
Enjoy some home-made and organic soup of the day in the Pepper Pot restaurant on the second floor of the **Powerscourt Townhouse** (➤ 77) shopping centre.

Getting Your Bearings

The southwestern district is the least picturesque part of the city centre, but the most fascinating from an historic perspective. It includes a wealth of sights which, when pieced together, tell the story of Dublin from the very first Celtic settlement in the fifth century to the present day. It was here, according to legend, that St Patrick started converting the Irish to Christianity; where the Vikings created their small settlement of *Dubh Linn* in AD841; and where the medieval walled city of Dublin developed.

This area includes some of the city's most magnificent buildings, notably the two medieval cathedrals of St Patrick and Christ Church, and Dublin Castle, the focus and foothold of the English in Ireland for more than 700 years.

To the west of the medieval core you will find a part of Dublin that has changed relatively little over the years: the shadow-laden cobbled streets of the Liberties district; the enormous 19th-century warehouses of the Guinness Brewery, where the air is heady with the smell of roasting barley; and Kilmainham, Europe's best-preserved 18th-century prison and a veritable shrine to those who suffered in the bitter struggle for Irish freedom.

In contrast, to the east are the popular outdoor cafes and watering-holes of Temple Bar, once a derelict dockland area but now the most happening part of town and a hive of activity night and day.

TOP 10

City Hall seen along Parliament Street

At Your Leisure

Southside West

The Perfect Day

If you're not quite sure where to begin your travels, this itinerary recommends a practical and enjoyable day in the western part of Southside, taking in some of the best places to see. For more information see the main entries (▶ 58–79).

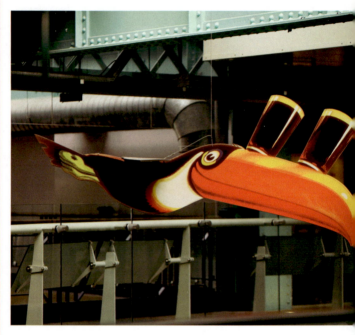

⊕ 9:30am
Start at ✪ **Kilmainham Gaol** (▶ 58), a grim, grey building steeped in Dublin's turbulent history. Not only does it provide an insight into what it was like to be confined in one of the forbidding cells, but it also documents some of the most heroic and tragic events in Ireland's emergence as a modern independent nation.

⊕ 11:30am
Hail a taxi and head eastwards to James's Gate, site of the massive Guinness Brewery – a 26ha (64-acre) sprawl of industry which on its own churns out more than 2.5 million pints a day. Learn how it's produced at the state-of-the-art ✪ **Guinness Storehouse** (above; ▶ 61).

⊕ 1:00pm
Spend your lunch break tucking into a hearty portion of Irish stew and sipping a perfect pint of the "black stuff" in one of three sky-high bars at the top of the Guinness Storehouse, while surveying the Brewery and the cityscape laid out seven storeys below.

🕑 2:00pm

Trace the city's early history at either the medieval exhibitions of **14 Dublinia** (above; ➤ 75) or ⭐**St Patrick's** (➤ 65), combined with a glance at the internal glories of **15 Christ Church Cathedral** (➤ 76), the city's first stone building, constructed in 1038. For a complete historical overview of the area's unique heritage, try the walking tour (➤ 156) and, if you have time, take a peek into the courtyard of ⭐**Dublin Castle** (➤ 70) – a mish-mash of buildings of various periods which served as the headquarters of the British Administration until 1922 when it was handed over to the Irish Free State.

🕓 4:00pm

There's just time before the shops close (6pm) to exercise your credit cards at the stylish **17 Powerscourt Townhouse** (➤ 77), which occupies a converted 18th-century mansion, or in the chic boutiques in the surrounding streets.

🕕 6:00pm

Head to ⭐**Temple Bar** (➤ 68), Dublin's buzzing entertainment district and artistic quarter, where you're sure to find live music and great *craic* at its dozens of thriving restaurants, cafes, pubs and clubs. Temple Bar Market takes place on Saturdays (➤ 84). Good traditional Dublin pubs? Try the **Palace Bar** on Fleet Street (➤ 85).

⭐3 Kilmainham Gaol

On first impression, the dark, dank cells of an empty old prison may seem an unlikely place to visit. Yet Kilmainham Gaol provides a moving insight into some of the most profound and inspirational themes of modern Irish history. Many of the country's heroes were incarcerated here during the 140 years following the gaol's construction in 1796. Today it stands preserved as a powerful symbol of that long and bitter struggle for independence.

Historic Moments

The chilling grey fortress of Kilmainham Gaol has been compared to the Bastille in Paris. Indeed, its construction was inspired by the fear of French revolutionary ideals spreading to Ireland, a fear that ultimately found expression in the 1798 Rebellion. Before long the rebel leaders of the United Irishmen and the participants of the insurrection filled the cells. In 1803, following his abortive rebellion, **Robert Emmet** was imprisoned here together with 200 of his supporters. An heroic champion of Irish liberty, even on the night before his public hanging Emmet made a defiant, patriotic speech at his trial to inspire later generations of freedom fighters.

In 1866 the **Fenian suspects** (►60) were imprisoned here. In 1881 **Charles Stewart Parnell** (►127) was kept here for six months, during which time he signed the No Rent Manifesto and negotiated the Kilmainham Treaty with British prime minister William Gladstone from his prison cell. In 1914 the gaol was converted into barracks to accommodate the extra troops recruited for World War I. It was reopened two years later to receive insurgents of the **1916 rebellion** (see panel). After the Easter Rising, the **War of Independence** and the subsequent **Civil War** kept gaolers and executioners busy until the release of the final prisoner, **Éamon de Valera** (►22). It marked the end of his second internment at Kilmainham: he had narrowly escaped execution in 1916 because he was an American citizen. Later he became both head of government and president of Ireland.

> ### THE 1916 EASTER RISING
> All those sentenced to death for their part in the Easter Rising were executed in the stone-breaking yard of Kilmainham Gaol (except Roger Casement, who was hanged in London). The list included Pádraic Pearse, Joseph Plunkett, Tom Clarke and James Connolly who, wounded and unable to stand up, was strapped to a chair before being shot. Plunkett came before the firing squad just two hours after he had married Grace Gifford in the prison chapel. These public executions turned the 14 leaders into martyrs and did more than anything else to turn the tide of public opinion against British rule in Ireland. For this reason, Kilmainham Gaol holds a significant place in people's hearts today.

The Gaol Today

Following the closure of the prison, the building lay abandoned for decades and fell into decay. However, because of its exceptional historical interest, restoration work began in 1960 to preserve the largest remaining decommissioned

Cells radiate around a central hall

prison in Europe. Entrance today is by guided tour only.

The grim, grey facade of the building sets the tone for your visit as you enter through the sinister thick door with a spy hatch that greeted the unfortunate prisoners at the start of their sentence. Above the door, five entwined serpents cast in bronze were known as the **Five Devils of Kilmainham**, and above that is the **gibbet** where public hangings took place. The main body of the prison – with its severe metal stairways, chicken-wired galleries and bleak rows of cells – contains numerous **display cases** with documents and mementoes of the inmates which retell the story of the struggle for Irish nationalism, along with various locks, shackles and the gallows. The **guided tour** leads you through the fearful dungeons, corridors and Spartan cells that still evoke a shudder and a sense of the building's tragic history as it portrays the tales of the people and forces that shaped modern Ireland.

TAKING A BREAK

Enjoy a light lunch at **The Tea Rooms** on the premises of Kilmainham Gaol.

✚ 186 B4
✉ Inchicore Road, Kilmainham, D8
☎ 01 453 5984; www.heritageireland.ie
🕐 Apr–Sep daily 9:30–6;
Oct–Mar Mon–Sat 9:30–5:30, Sun 10–6
🚌 69 (from Aston Quay), hop-on, hop-off tour buses 🚊 LUAS: Suir Road
🎫 €6

THE FENIAN BROTHERHOOD

The Fenians were members of an Irish nationalist secret militant group, which was formed in a Dublin timberyard on St Patrick's Day in 1858, and especially active in Ireland, America and Britain during the 1860s. The Irish Republican Brotherhood (and later the IRA) developed from it, and, in 1905, one of its members, Arthur Griffith, went on to found the Irish nationalist party, Sinn Féin (We Ourselves).

A narrow corridor in the gaol

INSIDER INFO

Insider Tip

- Ask the guide to **shut you into one of the cells** to experience the grim reality of prison life here.
- If you're pressed for time, skip the **audio-visual presentation**, which is the least gripping part of the tour.

★4 Guinness Storehouse

For centuries, Guinness has been synonymous with Ireland, and more particularly with Dublin. The stories of the city and Arthur Guinness's James's Gate Brewery are inextricably linked, and now one of Dublin's most popular and ambitious attractions is located in the heart of the brewery. This ultra-modern museum provides a fascinating insight into the operations and history of the making of Guinness and a shrine to the pint of what James Joyce so memorably called "the wine of the country".

The Guinness Storehouse by night

Early History

Guinness is one of Dublin's greatest success stories. In 1759 Arthur Guinness, a brewer's son aged 34, took over a small disused brewery here and leased it for 9,000 years at IR£45 a year. (The lease today is enshrined in the floor at the centre of the reception area of the museum.) After a short period of brewing ale he began to produce "porter" – a dark beer containing roasted barley – which rapidly achieved widespread popularity throughout Ireland and also captured a share of the market in Britain. Other Dublin brewers also began to make porter, so Arthur decided to brew a stronger beer called "extra stout porter", which involved burning the hops during production to provide a distinctively bitter taste. Thus he created the "black gold" of Guinness – a rich, black liquid, topped with a "foamous" (as James Joyce described it), creamy head. It soon

became known as "stout", and its fame spread quickly. It is now consumed in many countries around the world. Arthur died in 1803, but he had 21 children (only 10 survived to adulthood) and the brewery has remained in the hands of the Guinness family ever since.

There was no shortage of competition for the Guinness factory in the 19th century, with 55 breweries producing beer in Dublin alone, but there were plenty of consumers too. It is said that ale-houses formed one-third of the total number of houses in the city. Drinking ale was a regular part of everyday life. It was safer to drink than the contaminated water of Dublin, and even babies were given weak ale instead of milk. It is reckoned that at one point, more than a third of Dublin's population depended on the Guinness Brewery for its income – easy to believe, if you view the site from the north bank of the Liffey. From here, it looks like a great, sprawling metropolis, a city within a city. It even had special trains linking it with nearby Heuston Station, barges that ferried barrels up the river and its own fleet of steamers.

By the time the company was floated in 1886, Guinness had grown from its original site of 1.6ha (4 acres) to become the largest brewery in the world (now Europe), with more than 2,600 employees. Today it covers some 26ha (64 acres) of the city centre, with its own water and electricity supply. It produces more than 2.5 million pints every day, of which half are drunk in Ireland, and exports more beer than any other single brewery anywhere, to 120 countries.

Top Attraction

The Guinness Storehouse is one of the city's top attractions. A heady smell of roasting barley greets visitors as they approach the entrance and continue past an imposing skyline of chimneys, warehouses and vat-houses to the heart of the largest brewery in Europe. The museum building is a spectacle in itself, housed on seven floors of a magnificently converted warehouse. Instead of gutting the relics of the old industrial building and processes, the architects have made them a feature, with great steel girders left uncovered, and the defunct machines and vats left where they were or incorporated into the exhibition. The interior shell has been totally exposed; rising through the middle of the space is a series of rounded balconies that form the shape of a mighty pint glass.

Southside West

The **museum** starts dramatically with display cases containing the various ingredients for Guinness, situated beneath a pounding waterfall. It is a simple recipe based on Irish-grown barley, hops, yeast and water which, contrary to popular belief, comes from the Grand Canal and not the River Liffey. The next few levels of the exhibition follow the course of a pint of Guinness through the **traditional brewing process**, complete with sounds and smells: the clanking, gurgling, hissing and rumbling of the machines; the voices of the men who worked here; and the heavy, sleepy smell of hops, hot metal, sweat and steam. You can even walk inside the copper stills and the vats, capable of holding 405,000 litres – that's 713,000 pints of Guinness!

Bottles bearing labels from different years

Other **smaller sections** are devoted to Arthur Guinness (► 21); **cooperage**; **transportation**, where an original Guinness steam locomotive and models of ships, barges, carts and trains illustrate the different modes of beer export; and **advertising** through the ages.

Finally, lifts at the top of the building take you up to "the head on the building's internal pint", to the breathtaking surroundings of the seventh-floor **Gravity Bar**. They say that Guinness doesn't travel well; that it never tastes the same drunk outside Dublin or from a can. Where better place to enjoy a glass than at the brewery itself?

Insider Tip

TAKING A BREAK

The Guinness Storehouse has three bars: the **Arthur's Bar** where you can simply relax with a pint of the "black stuff"; the **Silroy's Bar**, offering contemporary Irish dishes; and the **Gravity Bar**, serving a complimentary pint of Guinness accompanied by striking city views.

➕ 187 E4　✉ St James's Gate, D8
☎ 01 408 4800; www.guinness-storehouse.com
🕐 Daily 9:30–5 (Jul–Aug last admission 6pm)　🚌 123 (from O'Connell Street); tour buses also stop here　🚊 LUAS: James's　💶 €20

INSIDER INFO

- The **admission fee** includes a complimentary pint of Guinness (in the Gravity Bar).
- There is an excellent Guinness **gift shop** on the ground floor.
- The **advertising section** consists of a huge display of ads over the decades, starting with the first, most celebrated one, produced in 1929, announcing "Guinness is Good for You".
- The **Cooperage**: an audio-visual display showing how barrels were made in the 1950s. If you are pressed for time then see the other exhibits first.
- The **Learning Centre**: an entire floor devoted to teaching bartenders how to pull the perfect pint.

St Patrick's Cathedral

The handsome Cathedral of St Patrick is Dublin's second great Protestant cathedral, the national church and the largest church in Ireland. More than any other building in Ireland it embodies the history and heritage of Irish people of all backgrounds from the earliest times to the present day.

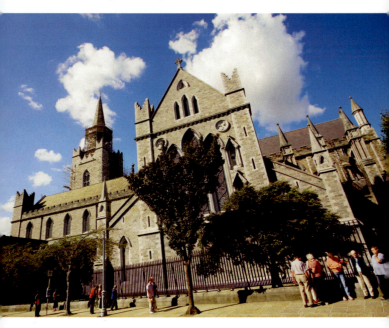

The current 19th-century cathedral stands on an ancient site

According to legend, the cathedral was built near a small well in which St Patrick is believed to have baptized his converts to Christianity in the fifth century. Today, a stone in St Patrick's Park, beside the cathedral, marks the site of the original well. It is said that the saint caused the well to spring from the earth and, for centuries, the water was thought to possess miraculous healing properties. Because of this association with St Patrick, a small wooden church probably existed here as early as AD450. The Normans built a stone church on the site in 1191, which was rebuilt in the early 13th century. However, by the 19th century the church had fallen into a poor state of repair and much of it was rebuilt in a major restoration project financed by the Guinness family. Sadly, little of the original building remains.

St Patrick's Cathedral

Cathedral Treasures

St Patrick's most celebrated dean was the passionate social reformer, satirist and author of *Gulliver's Travels*, **Jonathan Swift** (➤ 17). He served here from 1713 to 1745 and is buried under a brass plaque set into the nave floor just to the right of the entrance desk. His self-penned epitaph, translated from the Latin, reads: "Here is laid the body of Jonathan Swift, Doctor of Divinity, Dean of this Cathedral Church, where fierce indignation can no longer rend the heart,/Go travellers and imitate, if you can, this earnest and dedicated Champion of Liberty."

Buried alongside Swift is his companion "Stella" (Esther Johnson), with whom he had a long and apparently platonic relationship. His death mask, chair and writing table are also on display, together with his pulpit.

Other **noteworthy treasures** include the 17th-century monument of the Boyle family, Ireland's largest organ, and a rare collection of memorials to Irish soldiers killed in British Empire wars. In the 13th-century **Lady Chapel** you can see the high-backed chair upon which William III sat when he attended a service here on 6 July 1690, after the Battle of the Boyne.

TAKING A BREAK

Just up the hill from the cathedral, a tiny relaxing cafe called **Bite of Life** (55 Patrick Street, D8; tel: 01 454 2949; www.biteoflife.com; open Mon–Sun 9–4) serves delicious coffees, home-made soups, sandwiches, rolls and cakes.

➕ 190 B1
✉ St Patrick's Close, D8
☎ 01 453 9472; www.stpatrickscathedral.ie
🕐 Mar–Oct Mon–Fri 9:30–5, Sat 9–6, Sun 9–10:30, 12:30–2:30, 4:30–6; Nov–Feb Mon–Sat 9:30–5, Sun 9–10:30, 12:30–2:30
🚌 50, 54A, 56A (Eden Quay) 🎫 €6

Heraldic banners of the knights of the Order of St Patrick overhang the choir stalls along the nave of the cathedral, with the altar beyond

★6 Temple Bar

Upbeat, bohemian and youthful, Temple Bar is the city's cultural quarter – a lively district of contemporary arts and entertainment, with some of the best bars, pubs and clubs in town.

The compact, pedestrian-friendly district of Temple Bar owes its name to Sir William Temple, who purchased the land in the 16th century. By the mid-17th century it was Dublin's busiest marine trading area, with a bustling harbour at Wellington Quay. (The term "bar" means "riverside path".) But as the average tonnage of ships increased over the decades, the low depth of the Liffey here forced the docks eastwards, and Temple Bar was abandoned for nearly 200 years.

A New Look

It was the naming of Dublin as European City of Culture in 1991 that spurred the rejuvenation of Temple Bar, and the district has been at the epicentre of Dublin's revival ever since. The area has undergone a radical transformation: the former warehouses and merchant's houses clustered along the cobweb of narrow, cobbled streets have been rediscovered, renovated and redesigned with elements of bold contemporary architecture. Now it is the social heart of Dublin, and a gathering place for Dublin youth.

The Oliver St John Gogarty in the heart of Temple Bar

One of the main trademarks of Temple Bar is the large number of cafes, restaurants, pubs and bars (➤ 84), many of which host live music ranging from fiddle sessions to up-and-coming Dublin rock bands. The area is also renowned for its nightlife. In the 1990s Temple Bar was in danger of sinking beneath a tide of wild stag parties and drunken weekenders drawn here from across Europe. However, the balance was restored with the introduction

Insider Tip

INSIDER INFO

Insider Tip

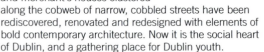

A **programme of free events** takes place day and evening. Full details are available from the Temple Bar Cultural Information Centre (➤ 69).

of a summer programme of free arts events, including street theatre and open-air markets. Now, there's always something exciting happening, whether it's street entertainment, a music recital or an outdoor film-screening at Meeting House Square, or special events like the Temple Bar Fleadh (pronounced "flah") in March or the summer festival featuring circus, music, dance and visual arts (➤ 27). As Temple Bar is also the trendiest part of town, it also boasts a variety of unusual craft shops, independent boutiques and markets (➤ 82).

Cultural Centres

There is a wide range of innovative cultural centres including the **Temple Bar Gallery** (5–9 Temple Bar), the **Graphic Studio Gallery** (off Cope Street), and the **Gallery of Photography** (Meeting House Square), all showing works by young artists and photographers; the **National Photographic Archive** (Meeting House Square), housing the photographic collection of the National Library of Ireland (➤ 110); the **Irish Film Institute** and **Irish Film Archive** (6 Eustace Street), showing independent and foreign films as well as lectures and seminars; 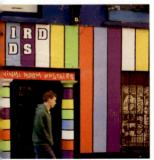 **The Ark** (11a Eustace Street), Europe's first cultural centre for children, including an outdoor theatre, **Cultivate** (15–19 Essex Street West), a sustainable living centre; and **Project Arts Centre** (39 East Essex Street), with two theatres and a gallery.

TAKING A BREAK

Temple Bar possesses the greatest density of pubs and eateries in Dublin (➤ 80 and 84 for a selection).

Temple Bar is a good place to find vintage clothes and record shops

✚ 191 D3

Cultural Information Centre
✉ 12 East Essex Street, D2 ☎ 01 677 2255 🕐 Mon–Fri 9–5:30, Sat 10–5:30, Sun noon–3 🚌 All city centre buses 🚉 DART: Tara Street

★9 Dublin Castle

Dublin Castle marks the centre of historic Dublin. For over 700 years it was the headquarters of English rule in Ireland, and Dubliners would joke about the figure of Justice over the main entrance – that she had turned her back on the city. Today, the hotch-potch of architectural styles, the faded brick facades and the tranquil atmosphere of the courtyards belie the turbulent history once enacted here.

The castle stands on a strategic ridge above the junction of the River Liffey and its tributary, the Poddle. It is thought that an early Gaelic ring fort stood on this site, and later a Viking fortress. The building of a medieval castle, with moat, drawbridge and portcullis, was ordered in 1204 by England's King John, who required "a castle…for the custody of our treasure…for the use of justice in the city and if it needs be, for the city's defence with good dykes and strong walls." The castle has been the seat and symbol of secular power in Ireland from that time until 1922 when it was handed over to the Irish Free State.

Throughout its lifetime as a British stronghold, various unsuccessful attempts were made to take the castle by such figures as Edward Bruce (died 1318), Silken Thomas Fitzgerald (1513–37) and Robert Emmet (1778–1803), and in World War I it was used as a military hospital. A further attempt was made to capture it by the Irish Volunteers in the 1916 Rising. They gained entry to the

Dublin Castle and adjoining buildings – a jumble of architectural styles

castle grounds and held out for a day on the roof of City Hall before being captured. Once the rebellion had been suppressed, their leader, James Connolly (▶ 22), was held in one of the State Rooms before being taken to Kilmainham to face execution.

The Castle Today

Today's ensemble of buildings no longer looks like a castle, having been largely rebuilt in the 18th century as the political, judicial and punitive centre for the Crown, with assembly courts and offices clustered around two

DUBH LINN

The city owes its name to the "black pool" (*Dubh Linn* in Irish) originally located on the site of the present castle garden. The pool was formed by the River Poddle, which still flows beneath the castle. The Vikings once moored their longboats here, and the Normans diverted the flow of the river to make their moat.

courtyards, together with luxurious ceremonial apartments to accommodate the British viceroys. Some of the rebuilding was unplanned, for a fire spread to the Powder Tower where the gunpowder was stored, blowing up a large part of the castle.

Little survives of the medieval castle that once occupied the site of today's Upper Castle Yard. The only visible remains are the base of the **Bermingham Tower**, the curtain wall beneath St Patrick's Hall, the foundations of the Powder Tower to the north, and the lower walls of the **Record Tower**, which today houses the **Garda Museum**. Alongside the tower in the Lower Yard, the small, neo-Gothic **Chapel Royal** was built in 1807 on the site of an

Southside West

earlier chapel with carved stone likenesses of British dignitaries outside and elaborate wood- and plasterwork within, some of which is painted to resemble stone.

Upper Castle Yard contains the castle's principal buildings. The State Apartments occupy the entire southern side of the yard and are used for such grand occasions as the inauguration of the president,

as well as official entertainment, European summit meetings, peace talks and other State functions. They are sometimes even used as a hotel for heads of state and high-risk VIPs when they visit for discussions on the tangled issues of Ireland. A guided tour leads you through numerous palatial 18th-century rooms decorated with sumptuous period furnishings, vast Waterford chandeliers, hand-tufted Donegal carpets and magnificent Adam fireplaces.

At the end of the tour, the *pièce de résistance* is a visit to the **Undercroft** several metres below the yard level. Here you can see part of the original Viking fortress, the original city wall with its roughly hewn arches where the moat once flowed, and even a glimpse of the River Poddle, now underground.

Near the entrance to the State Apartments, the splendid octagonal clock tower is the site of one of the castle's most puzzling crimes. It was from here, in 1907, that the Irish Crown jewels were stolen while under a heavy guard. To this day they have never been found.

Right: The Bedford Tower at night

TAKING A BREAK

Insider Tip

The **Queen of Tarts**, opposite the castle (Cork Hill, Dame Street, D2; tel: 01 670 7499, open Mon–Fri 8–7, Sat, Sun 9–7), is something of a cult place to enjoy hot savoury tarts,

The Drawing Room is among the fine State Apartments

THE CHESTER BEATTY LIBRARY

The well-organized Chester Beatty Library – consisting of around 22,000 rare and precious manuscripts, books, miniature paintings and objects from Western, Middle Eastern and Far Eastern cultures – was bequeathed to the Irish nation in 1956 by Sir Alfred Chester Beatty and is considered among the most impressive collections of its kind in the world. It can be visited Mar–Oct Mon–Fri 10–5, Sat 11–5, Sun 1–5; Nov–Feb Tue–Sat 10–5, Sun 11–5. Free guided tours of the collection take place on Wed at 1pm and Sun at 3pm and 4pm; tel: 01 407 0750; www.cbl.ie.

wholesome sandwiches, salads and a huge selection of cakes and sweet tarts. Try the Baileys chocolate chip cheesecake.

190 C2
Dame Street, D2
01 645 8813; www.dublincastle.ie
Mon–Sat 10–4:45, Sun noon–4:45; closed during State business
49, 54A, 56A, 77 (from Eden Quay), 123 (from O'Connell Street)
€6

INSIDER INFO

- The **tour of the State Apartments** includes the Throne Room, the richly decorated Ballroom (known as St Patrick's Hall), the Wedgwood Room, the Apollo Room, which has a sumptuous stuccoed ceiling, the circular Gothic-style Supper Room, and the 30m-long (100ft) Picture Gallery, which houses a collection of portraits of former viceroys, their coronets surmounting the gilt frames.
- The ceiling fresco in **St Patrick's Hall**, depicting scenes from Irish history, is considered the most important painted ceiling in Ireland.
- The **Garda Museum**, records the history of the police force – this is one for those with a specialist interest and those with plenty of time.

At Your Leisure

11 Irish Museum of Modern Art (IMMA)

The Irish Museum of Modern Art is Ireland's leading national institution of modern and contemporary art, where the work of major international figures is juxtaposed with the latest trends of up-and-coming local artists.

The collections are housed in the Royal Hospital in Kilmainham, considered by many to be the finest 17th-century building in Ireland. Designed by Sir William Robinson in 1684, and styled on Les Invalides in Paris, with a spacious quadrangle and elegant classical symmetry, it was a home for retired soldiers for almost 250 years until 1922. Later, it was used by the British as an army barracks. Only in 1986 did the Irish government restore the long-abandoned building at a cost of IR£12 million. It reopened its doors as the Irish Museum of Modern Art in 1991. Now its stark grey-and-white interior provides a striking backdrop for the permanent collection of Irish and international 20th-century art, as well as regular temporary exhibitions and workshops. Look out for The Madden Arnholz Collection, Old Master prints by the likes of Rembrandt, Hogarth and Goya, and **The City Drawings**, hundreds of drawings of cities around the world by leading Irish artist Kathy Prendergast.

A sculpture displayed in the grounds of the Irish Museum of Modern Art

✚ 186 C4
✉ Royal Kilmainham Hospital, Kilmainham, D8
☎ 01 612 9900; www.imma.ie
🕐 Tue–Fri 11:30–5:30, Sat 10–5,
Sun and public hols noon–5:30.
Guided tours: Wed 1:15, Sat, Sun 2:30
🚌 13, 40, 79, 79A, 123, 145 🎟 Free

12 St Audoen's Churches

The Protestant **Church of St Audoen** is the only remaining medieval parish church in Dublin. It stands on the site of a Celtic chapel dedicated to St Columba, the patron saint of poets and one of Ireland's best-loved saints. Its 12th-century tower is believed to be the oldest in Ireland, and its three bells and nave date from the 15th century. In the porch, an early Christian gravestone known as the "Lucky Stone" – the subject of many strange stories – has been here since the 13th century. The churchyard is bounded by a restored section of old city walls. Behind the church, St Audoen's Arch is the only remaining gateway of the medieval city.

Next door to old St Audoen stands 19th-century **St Audoen's**

Arran Quay
Usher's Quay
Irish Museum of Modern Art (IMMA)
11
Bridgefoot St
St Audoen's Churches
High St
12 Dublinia
14
Thomas Street
13
Tailor's Hall

Catholic Church. Its Great Bell is better known as *The Liberator*, after Daniel O'Connell (➤ 21). It rang to announce his release from prison and tolled on the day of his funeral. The church's congregation had dropped to around 200 a week until it became home to the Polish chaplaincy; now 7,000 mostly Eastern European churchgoers attend Mass.

✚ 190 A2 ✉ Corn Market, High Street, D2
☎ 01 677 0088; www.heritageireland.com
🕐 May–Oct daily 9:30–5:30,
(last admission 45 mins before closing)
🎫 Free 🚌 Bus 78a, 123

🄱 Tailor's Hall

Dublin's only remaining guildhall, the Tailor's Hall, was built in 1706, making it the oldest guildhall in Ireland. In its heyday it was used by a variety of traders including hosiers, saddlers and tailors. It also hosted political gatherings – notably the illegal "Back Lane Parliament" meetings of the Society of United Irishmen, founded towards the end of the 18th century by Theobald Wolfe Tone (➤ 21), the middle-class Protestant attorney and father of Irish Republicanism. Since 1985, it has been the home of An Taisce – the Irish National Trust.

✚ 190 A2
✉ Back Lane, off Christchurch Place, D2
🕐 Closed to the public

🄸🄳 👫 Dublinia

This state-of-the-art heritage centre – named Dublinia after the first known recording of the city on a map in 1540 – covers Dublin's turbulent history from the arrival of the Anglo-Normans in 1170 to the reign of Henry VIII and the closure of the monasteries in 1540. Thrilling life-sized street scenes and audio-visual displays on the ground floor, combined with artefacts from the National Museum of Ireland upstairs and a 1:300 scale model of the city, provide an exciting insight into medieval life. There's a Medieval Fair where you can try juggling and brass-rubbing, or dress up as a medieval knight. Kids love it. The displays are located in the old Synod Hall beside Christ Church Cathedral, and the visit concludes with a climb to the top of St Michael's Tower for a bird's-eye view of the medieval city.

Insider Tip

✚ 190 B2
✉ St Michael's Hill, D8
☎ 01 679 4611; www.dublinia.ie
🕐 Mar–Sep 10–6:30; Oct–Feb 10–5:30
🚌 49, 49A, 54A, 123 🎫 €8.50, children €5.50

A re-created boat in the Viking World exhibit at Dublinia

Lights illuminate the crypt at Christ Church Cathedral

🄵 Christ Church Cathedral

Christ Church Cathedral was the first stone building to be erected in Dublin. It replaced an earlier wooden church built in 1038 for Sitric Silkenbeard, the Norse king of Dublin. The cathedral was commissioned in 1172 by the Anglo-Norman conqueror of Dublin, Richard FitzGilbert de Clare, the Second Earl of Pembroke – more commonly known as "Strongbow" – for Archbishop Laurence O'Toole (who later became St Laurence, the patron saint of Dublin).

Over the centuries, the cathedral has been repeatedly restored and modified. In the mid-15th century, the cloisters were taken over by shops and the crypt became "tippling rooms for beer, wine and tobacco". Later, in the 19th century, the church was -completely remodelled by the architect George Street. Little remains of the cathedral's original Norman structure, except parts of the south transept and the crypt.

Inside the building, look for Strongbow's memorial in the nave

Flamboyant architecture – under the central dome of City Hall

and the heart of St Laurence, kept in a 13th-century metal casket in the chapel of St Laud. Unique in Ireland for its scale and size, the crypt is almost as large as the upper church and full of -fascinating relics and statuary. The most prized pieces, which form part of an exhibition entitled Treasures of Christ Church, include a silver plate gifted to the cathedral by King William III in 1697. There's also a glass case containing the mummified bodies of a cat and rat, found in the 1860s. The rat was trapped in an organ pipe and the cat, in hot pursuit, got jammed just 15cm (6in) away from its prey.

✚ 190 B2 ✉ Christchurch Place, D8
☎ 01 677 8099; www.christchurchcathedral.ie
🕐 Mar, Oct Mon–Sat 9–6, Sun 12:30–2:30, 4:30–6; Apr–Sep Mon–Fri 9–6, Sun 12:30–2:30, 4:30–7; Nov–Feb Mon–Fri 9–5, Sun 12:30–2:30
🚌 13, 27, 40, 49, 77A, 123 🎫 €6

🄸 City Hall

Immediately after its construction in 1769, Dublin's City Hall was hailed as an architectural masterpiece. Originally designed by Thomas Cooley to house the Royal Exchange at a time when a revolutionary wind was sweeping through Georgian Dublin, the exterior marked the introduction of neoclassicism to Ireland and also set a new trend for copper-covered domes (see also the Custom House, ▶ 136, and the Four Courts, ▶ 133). One of Cooley's assistants was James Hoban, who was to make his name a decade later by winning the com-

Powerscourt Townhouse – a stylish shopping centre fashioned from a grand Georgian mansion

petition to design the White House in Washington DC.

Today the City Hall contains the offices of the Dublin Corporation and a multimedia exhibition tracing the -evolution of Ireland's capital city from the early developments to the present day. Look out for the marble statues of important political figures, such as Daniel O'Connell (➤ 21) and Henry Grattan (➤ 93), and also for the city's coat of arms and motto *Obedientia Civium Urbis Felicitas* (Happy the City Where Citizens Obey), which is depicted in mosaic set into the floor of the dazzling, light-filled rotunda.

The rotunda's dramatic space makes it a popular setting for public

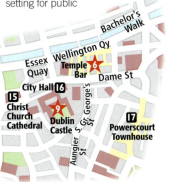

and private events, from dinners and fashion shows to Halloween parties and other celebrations.

🕂 190 C3 ✉ Cork Hill, Dame Street, D2
☎ 01 222 2204; www.dublincity.ie
🕓 Mon–Sat 10–5:15, Sun 2–5:15
🚌 27, 54A, 56A, 77A, 123, 150 🎫 €4

🔢 Powerscourt Townhouse

This grand Georgian mansion was designed by Robert Mack (the architect of Grattan Bridge), in 1774 as the city pad of Viscount Powerscourt, whose principal residence was in County Wicklow (➤ 148). It became a drapery warehouse in the 1830s, but today it has been converted into a sophisticated shopping mall (➤ 82), cleverly combining the original facade, the grand mahogany staircase and some splendid stucco work with imaginative, modern interior design. Weary shoppers can rest their feet at Pygmalion Café in the floor-to-ceiling atrium; the upper balconies and corridors lead to an upmarket mix of independent boutiques, antique jewellers, and several other eateries and bars.

Insider Tip

🕂 191 D2 ✉ William Street South, D2
ℹ️ www.powerscourtcentre.com 🕓 Mon–Fri 10–6 (Thu until 8), Sat 9–6, Sun noon–6

Southside West

ST VALENTINE

Various theories explain St Valentine's connection with lovers: according to folklore, birds choose their mates on his feast day, 14 February; this date also coincides with the ancient Roman fertility festival of *Lupercalia*. Whatever the reason, he has been invoked by lovers since medieval times. His remains are in Whitefriar Street Carmelite Church (► 78).

🔞 Whitefriar Street Carmelite Church

St Valentine, the third-century patron saint of lovers (► 79), died in Rome, but his remains were brought to Ireland in 1836 and now lie in a shrine to the right of the high altar in this church. Built on the site of a former Carmelite priory, it also contains an unusual oak statue of the Virgin (Our Lady of Dublin). The only survivor of its kind following the sacking of Ireland's monasteries during the Reformation, it was found in a second-hand shop.

✚ 190 C1 B56 Aungier Street, D2
☎ 01 475 8821; www.whitefriarstreetchurch.ie
🕐 Mon, Wed–Fri 7:30–6, Tue 7:30–9
🚌 9, 16, 49, 65, 68, 83, 122 💶 Free

🔞 Marsh's Library

Marsh's Library, Ireland's oldest public library, was founded in 1707 by Archbishop Narcissus Marsh, an avid collector of rare books and manuscripts. Designed by Sir William Robinson, the bookcases contain a scholarly collection of some 25,000 leather-bound publications, mostly dating from the 16th to the 18th centuries. Among the most prized volumes is Jonathan Swift's annotated copy of Clarendon's *History of the Great Rebellion*.

Some of the books in the library are so precious that readers were locked in with them, in the three caged alcoves at the end of the gallery. The rarest books were chained to the walls to prevent anyone from "borrowing" them. The library holds occasional temporary exhibitions.

✚ 190 B1 ✉ St Patrick's Close, D8
☎ 01 454 3511; www.marshlibrary.ie
🕐 Mon, Wed–Fri 9:30–5, Sat 10–5
🚌 49, 54A, 56A (Eden Quay) 💶 €3

🔞 Irish Jewish Museum & Heritage Centre

There has been a Jewish community in Ireland for centuries. Following the end of the Napoleonic

The oak bookcases in Marsh's Library, Ireland's oldest public library

Wars, Jewish immigrants arrived from central Europe, but the main influx was between 1880 and 1910 when some 2,000 Jews settled here from eastern Europe. Although only a handful of Jews arrived during the Nazi period, the community peaked at around 5,500 in the late 1940s.

This museum has a fascinating collection of memorabilia relating to Irish-Jewish communities. The ground floor illustrates their com-

George Bernard Shaw's bedroom at Shaw's Birthplace

Interior of the synagogue at the Irish Jewish Museum and Heritage Centre

mercial, cultural and social life, including a late 19th-century kitchen depicting a Sabbath meal. Upstairs, the original synagogue is on view together with the Harold Smerling gallery of Jewish religious objects.

✚ 187 F3
✉ 3–4 Walworth Road (off Victoria Street), D8
☎ 01 453 1797; www.jewishmuseum.ie
🕐 May–Oct Sun–Thu 11–3:30; Nov–Apr Sun 10:30–2:30
🚌 9, 16, 68, 68A, 122 🎟 Free

21 Shaw's Birthplace

A simple wall plaque – "Author of many Plays" – marks the birthplace of George Bernard Shaw (1836–1950). His childhood home near the Grand Canal Bridge at Portobello has been restored to its domestic Victorian elegance providing a wonderful insight into

the life of the Shaw family. Here Shaw would drink "much tea out of brown delft left to 'draw' on the hob until it was pure tannin" at his mother's tea parties, as he began to gather the characters who would later populate his books.

At the age of 20, Shaw moved to London, where he achieved success with such plays as *Arms and the Man*, *Man and Superman*, *Saint Joan* and *Pygmalion*. In 1925 he was awarded the Nobel Prize for literature (► 16). Many of his works were banned in Ireland during his lifetime on the grounds of blasphemy or obscenity.

✚ 187 F3
✉ 33 Synge Street, D8
☎ 01 475 0854
🕐 Currently closed
🚌 16, 16A, 19, 19A, 122

Where to...
Eat and Drink

Bad Ass Café €

This Temple Bar institution, housed in a converted warehouse, serves pizzas, pastas, burgers, fajitas and salads in a buzzy, young environment. It is popular with all age groups, but especially with children who delight in the entertaining menu, the posters and cartoon pictures on the walls, and the theatrical displays of pizza-spinning and tossing. Breakfasts are served at weekends.

191 D3

✉ 9 Crown Alley, Temple Bar, D2

☎ 01 675 3005; www.badassdublin.com

🕐 Mon–Thu, Sun noon–midnight, Fri, Sat noon–1:30am

Butler's Chocolate Café €

This small, modern, non-smoking cafe-cum-chocolate-shop is the place to combine coffee-drinking with the taste and aroma of Butler's Irish handmade chocolates. Each hot drink comes with a complimentary chocolate. Milkshakes and frappés are available too.

191 D2

✉ 24 Wicklow Street, D2

☎ 01 671 0591; www.butlerschocolates.com

🕐 Mon–Fri 8–7 (Thu to 9), Sat 9–7, Sun 10:30–7

Café Mao €€

You'll find innovative Asian dishes (Thai, Malaysian, Indonesian, Japanese and Chinese), a funky crowd and a great buzz at this simple, stylish restaurant. Don't be put off by the no reservations policy or the wait for a table, as once you're seated the service is swift.

191 D2 ✉ 2–3 Chatham Row, D2

☎ 01 670 4899; www.mymao.ie

🕐 Mon–Wed noon–11, Thu, Fri noon–midnight, Sat, Sat 4–midnight

Chez Max €€

As if a decent Parisian bistro had been teleported to a quiet spot next to Dublin Castle, this deservedly popular French restaurant brings French classics – steak with bearnaise sauce, *poulet basquaise* – to a loyal crowd of regulars. Even midweek, Chez Max is full but the turnover is high thanks to the speedy service. The *moules frites* are delicious with a cold glass of Pouilly Fumé. Sinatra-esque music completes the picture.

190 C3 ✉ 1 Palace Street ☎ 01 633 7215; www.chezmax.ie 🕐 Mon–Fri 8am–midnight, Sat, Sun noon–midnight

Cleaver East €€€

This stylish restaurant offers modern Irish cuisine combined with Asian and other culinary traditions from around the world. The impressive interior is styled in dark tones and is classic and contemporary. Michelin-starred Oliver Dunne, who is also an Irish TV celebrity chef, heads up the kitchen.

190 C3 ✉ 6–8 East Essex Street, D2

☎ 01 531 3500; www.cleavereast.ie

🕐 Mon–Sat 5–10:30, Sun till 9:30

Coppinger Row €€–€€€

Imaginative Mediterranean cuisine cooked by professional chefs with years of experience. Choices include spinach gnocchi with Gorgonzola cream sauce, grilled sardines, beetroot risotto and grilled leg of lamb with thyme and red lentils.

<mark>Before you sit down to your meal, you should treat your-self to a cocktail at the bar.</mark> **Insider Tip**

Booking is advisable, also for the popular Sunday brunch. Casual, lively atmosphere.

➕ 191 D2
✉ Coppinger Row (off South William Street), D2
☎ 01 672 9884; www.coppingerrow.com
🕐 Mon–Sat 12:30–5:30, 6–11, Sun 12:30–4, 6–9

Elephant and Castle €–€€

The Elephant and Castle is cele-brated for its home-made burgers, giant bowls of salad and baskets of spicy chicken wings served all day. Hugely popular on Sundays for family brunch. Book ahead for peak-time dining.

➕ 191 D3 ✉ 18 Temple Bar, D2
☎ 01 679 3121; www.elephantandcastle.ie
🕐 Mon–Fri 8am–11:30pm, Sat, Sun 10:30am–11:30pm

Gallagher's Boxty House €

A hugely popular, traditional Irish restaurant specializing in "boxties" – griddled potato cakes wrapping up savoury fillings including beef and Beamish (stout), smoked fish, ba-con and cabbage – and other Irish fare. The pine dressers create a rustic atmosphere, and everything is served to the accompaniment of noisy chatter and Irish music.

➕ 191 D3 ✉ 20–21 Temple Bar, D2
☎ 01 677 2762; www.boxtyhouse.ie
🕐 Daily noon–10:30

Good World €–€€

Dim sum here is a real treat and duck and pork are house specialities. The place is always buzzing and perfect for medium to large groups. Ask for the "Chinese menu".

➕ 191 D2 ✉ 18 South Great George's Street, D2
☎ 01 677 5373 🕐 Daily noon–midnight

Hatch & Sons €

One of the few cafe-restaurants serving traditional Irish food. Besides the classic Irish stew, and beef and Guinness stew, they also offer blaas (soft floury bread rolls from Waterford) with tasty fillings, a variety of salads and delicious cakes.

➕ 191 E1 ✉ 15 St Stephen's Green, D2
☎ 01 661 00 75; www.hatchandsons.co
🕐 Mon, Tue, Fri 8–5, Wed, Thu till 9, Sat 9–6, Sun 10–5

Jules €€€

Dublin's top French restaurant – noted for its classic, seasonal cui-sine and seafood – is especially popular at lunchtimes with local business clientele. The exemplary service, candlelit tables and pristine white linen also make it an ideal choice for that romantic occasion.

➕ 190 C3 ✉ 74 Dame Street, D2
☎ 01 679 4555; www.veryjules.com
🕐 Tue–Sat noon–midnight

Leo Burdock's €

This is the oldest and best fish 'n' chip shop in town. Be prepared to wait…the freshest of fish and crispy chips are worth it.

➕ 190 C2 ✉ 2 Werburgh Street, D8
☎ 01 454 0306; www.leoburdocks.com
🕐 Daily noon–midnight

The Market Bar €–€€

Housed in an old factory this tapas bar and restaurant has a unique atmosphere with high skylights, original brick walls and polished floors. The menu has tasty treats such as French and Italian chees-es, marinated olives, smoked duck, nachos and calamari. On weekends you can meet friends from noon for a leisurely brunch of Serrano ham, *ciabatta* and Spanish sparkling wine. The wine list includes wines from Spain, Chile and – of course – sangria.

➕ 191 D2 ✉ 14A Fade Street, D2
☎ 01 613 9094; www.marketbar.ie
🕐 Mon–Thu noon–11:30, Fri, Sat till 1:30am, Sun noon–11

Monty's of Kathmandu €–€€

<mark>This is an absolute must for curry lovers.</mark> **Insider Tip** Try tender Nepalese lamb

masala or *jyogi bhat* (sage's rice and vegetable curry).

🟥 191 D3 ✉ 28 Eustace Street, D2
☎ 01 670 4911; www.montys.ie
🕐 Mon–Sat 5:30–11, Sun 5:30–10:30

Osteria Il Baccaro €€

In a cosy 17th-century cellar, this bustling taverna provides an authentic taste of Italy in the heart of Temple Bar, and serves regional dishes, such as wild venison stew with polenta or grilled Tuscan-style sausages, from a weekly changing menu. For a light meal, try the platters of cold cuts and cheeses with a carafe of cheap but decent house wine, served from the barrel.

🟥 191 D3
✉ Diceman's Corner, Meeting House Square, D2
☎ 01 671 4597; www.ilbaccarodublin.com
🕐 Mon–Thu, Sun 5:30–10:30, Fri, Sat 1–10:30

Pearl Brasserie €€€

Award-winning French-Irish cuisine and fine dining in the basement of a Georgian town house. The atmosphere is elegant and inviting, the small, à la carte menu is seasonal. Expect classic dishes such as prime Irish rib eye steak, artichoke gratin, smoked duck breast with truffled mashed potatoes as well as various vegetarian dishes and excellent, unusual desserts.

🟥 192 B1
✉ 20 Upper Merrion Street, D02XH98
☎ 01 661 3572; www.pearl-brasserie.com
🕐 Mon–Fri noon–2:30, 6–10:30, Sat 1–3, 6–10:30

The Pig's Ear €–€€

Expect the best of Irish cooking – soda bread, wild salmon, elderberry cream ice cream – all made with fresh local produce. Some tables have a view of Trinity College Park. At lunchtime there is an inexpensive two-course menu; in the evening the atmosphere is somewhat more elegant and formal.

🟥 191 E2 ✉ 4 Nassau Street, D2
☎ 01 670 3865; www.thepigsear.com
🕐 Mon–Sat noon–10

Silk Road Café €–€€

This airy cafe in the Chester Beatty Library's foyer offers a range of healthy home-cooked Middle Eastern and Mediterranean dishes. Enjoy moussaka, lamb with okra, falafel wraps or humous sandwiches and salads, then finish with a delicious sticky pastry.

🟥 190 C2
✉ Chester Beatty Library, 2 Palace Street, D2
☎ 01 407 0770; www.silkroadcafe.ie
🕐 Mon–Fri 10–4:30, Sat 11–4:30, Sun 1–4:30

Where to…
Shop

FASHION & BEAUTY

Powerscourt Townhouse (► 77), the former mansion of Viscount Powerscourt (entrances in Clarendon Street and William Street South, D2; www.powerscourtcentre.com; Mon–Fri 10–6 (Thu to 8), Sat 9–6, Sun noon–6) is now a mini-mall containing up-to-the-minute fashions in its many boutiques, including **The Loft Market** and **French Connection** (tel: 01 679 8199). Several small specialist shops, such as **Courtville Antiques** (www.courtvilleantiques.com) and **Delphi Antiques** (tel: 01 679 0331) sell handmade and antique jewellery. At **Austens Creations** (tel: 01 679 4256) you can watch the jeweller Patrick Flood creating pieces from platinum, silver and gold, which he adorns with the patterns of his Irish heritage.

Powerscourt's *pièce de résistance* is the **Design Centre on the second level** (www.designcentre.ie), containing the latest creations of more than 20 leading Irish fashion designers including John Rocha, Philip Treacy, Pauric Sweeney and Roisin Linnane, as well as international designers.

Insider Tip

Powerscourt also stages changing exhibitions by leading artists and craftspeople, while **Pzazz hair** and make-up salon offers a range of prices for men and women (tel: 01 679 4194; www.pzazz.ie).

Costume (10 Castle Market, D2; tel: 01 679 4188; www.costume dublin.ie) is selling smart separates and quirky labels, while **Susan Hunter's** tiny boutique (www.susan-hunterlingerie.ie) in the **Westbury Shopping Mall** is known for its range of sexy, self-indulgent lingerie.

In Temple Bar, join the trendsetters at funky clothing store **Urban Outfitters** (4 Cecilia Street, D2; tel: 01 670 6202; www.urbanoutfitters. com), spread over four levels. The **Whetstone Concept Salon** (7 Parliament Street, Temple Bar; tel: 01 677 1344; www.whetstone.ie) offers face and body treatments.

For the ultimate gift, go to **John Farrington** (32 Drury Street, D2; www.johnfarringtonantiques.com), following in the footsteps of U2's Adam Clayton, who allegedly spent IR£40,000 on an engagement ring for supermodel Naomi Campbell.

Feeling jaded after so much shopping? A visit to **Eve at The Grooming Rooms** (16 William Street South, D2; www.evebeauty.ie) will pep you up with its range of luxurious treatment packages.

VINTAGE CLOTHING

Dublin has always had a great choice of vintage and retro clothing stores. The best finds are at **George's Street Arcade** (South Great George's Street, D2; www.georgesstreetarcade.com), a covered arcade brimming with second-hand clothes and antique costume jewellery. Two great vintage clothes shops near the arcade are **Harlequin** (13 Castle Market, D2; tel: 01 671 0202), which stocks everything from Irish tweed to leather and Chinese silk jackets, and Dublin's oldest vintage clothing shop (50 Drury Street, D2; tel: 01 677

0406): **Jenny Vander** – a fascinating emporium filled with clothing and accessories from the 1940s and earlier. Charity shops are great places to spend a rainy afternoon seeking out a piece of classic clothing.

Insider Tip

ANTIQUES, ARTS & CRAFTS

The Francis Street area is renowned for its antiques. One of the top places is **O'Sullivan Antiques** (43–44 Francis Street, D8; www.osullivanantiques. com). Other gems include **Johnston Antiques** (69–70 Francis Street, D8; tel: 01 473 2384; www.johnston antiques.net), which specializes in art nouveau and art deco. In summer the **Ha'Penny Flea Market** (Ha'Penny Bridge, D2) is held every Saturday from noon to 6. The market has a wide variety of antiques and collectables.

Designyard (25 South Frederick, D2; www.designyardgallery.com) flies the flag for new Irish design. This centre for innovative decorative arts contains wonderful silver, jewellery, furniture, textiles, glass and ceramics by leading craftspeople.

Another specialist shop well worth a visit is **Daintree** (61 Camden Street, D2; www.daintree.ie), which sells beautiful diaries, notebooks and cards made by local artists, as well as a huge range of wedding stationery. It also has many unusual screenprinted papers, with samples from as far afield as Japan, France, Nepal and Mexico.

For a good arts and crafts market, seek out the **Designer Mart**, which comes to Cow's Lane each Saturday. It sells a wide range of crafts and clothing.

FOR CHILDREN

Jacadi Childrenswear (in 32 South King Street, D2; tel: 01 671 1418) has two floors of charming and elegant French children's fashion with prices to match.

FOOD

Dublin foodies spend their Wednesday and Saturday mornings at Meeting House Square in **Temple Bar** where the tiny artisan food stalls of the market sell a wonderful selection of bread, cakes and pastries, top-quality meat and fish, farmhouse cheeses, organic fruit and vegetables, olives, oils, chocolates, pâtés and terrines. Somewhat cheaper than the exclusive delis. There are also stalls selling hot drinks, juices and world foods which you can eat on the spot.

During the rest of the week, head for **Magills** (14 Clarendon Street, D2; tel: 01 671 3830), Dublin's best-loved delicatessen, which sells specialities such as Hick's Irish sausages, as well as fresh herbs, spices, exotic sauces, quality salamis and their own brand of home-made preserves.

Founded in 1983, the **Dublin Food Co-op** (12 Newmarket, D8; tel: 01 454 4258; www.dublinfood.coop) is a very successful organic and fair trade food market. Members of the co-op sell a selection of wholefoods that include fresh organic fruit and vegetables, Irish cheeses and wholemeal breads and pastries. You can have a chat with the friendly vendors as you enjoy an Ayurvedic tea or an organic coffee and a snack.

Fallon & Byrne (11–17 Exchequer Street, Dublin 2; www.fallonand byrne.com) is a delightful addition to Exchequer Street. The red-brick building comprises a food hall with a meat counter and a "proper grocer", a wine cellar and a restaurant. There are tempting treats, takeaway lunches from a sandwich counter, a fantastic choice of hampers and a great range of olive oils. The cheese counter concentrates on interesting Irish produce from artisan producers, as well as selling antipasti and ham. All the fish comes from sustainable and often local sources.

Where to...
Go Out

This area has some of the liveliest bars, pubs and clubs in Dublin. Between May and September it also has open-air theatre, puppetry and street musicians by day, while in the evening, dance, theatre, music and film are staged in Meeting House Square and Temple Bar Square.

BARS & PUBS

Temple Bar was originally envisaged as a cultural centre, but at night it is more like a social and entertainment park for the under-30s. By late evening, its bars and pubs are really rocking and most people are drunk, many of them tourists or weekenders on stag and hen outings from Britain. However, there are many places worth seeking out. Several hotels are worth visiting for their bars: there's the mature atmosphere of the **Octagon Bar** within the stylish Clarence Hotel (6–8 Wellington Quay, D2; tel: 01 407 0800; ► 44), owned by members of U2, thronged with beautiful people and famed for its cocktails.

The **Library Bar** of the Central Hotel (Exchequer Street, Dublin 2; tel: 01 679 7302) adds another layer of refinement with leather wing-back armchairs, an open fire and an occasional pianist.

South Great George's Street and its side streets have many bars; the coolest for some time, **The Globe** (11 South Great George's Street; www.globe.ie) combines a laid-back ambience with some of the best and most varied music in the city.

Hogan's (35 South Great George's Street; tel: 01 677 5904) is another trendy nightspot.

On the same street is **The George** (89 South Great George's Street, D2; www.thegeorge.ie), a late-night gay bar with "gay bingo" on Sundays.

Other possibilities are **The Norseman** (28E Essex Street; tel: 01 671 5135; www.norseman.ie) and **Fitzsimons** (21–22 Wellington Quay; tel: 01 677 9315) both in Essex Street East and **Bruxelles** (7 Harry Street, D2; www.bruxelles. ie), a fashionable, very loud watering-hole that attracts students and tourists.

Dublin's fashion leaders have moved beyond the touristy Temple Bar area, in particular to the area around William Street South. **Dakota** (9 William Street South, D2; www. dakotabar.com) serves pricey cocktails to smartly dressed thirtysome-things.

Close by, another chic and stylish place, and open till 2:30am, is **4 Dame Lane** (4 Dame Lane, D2; www.4damelane.ie; open till 3am).

Many such places have bar extensions until around 1:30–2am. Among the best is the **Capitol Lounge** (18–19 Lower Stephen's Street, D2; www.capitol.ie) – young, trendy, and with a superb upstairs cocktail bar.

To sample a traditional pub order a pint at the **Palace Bar** (21 Fleet Street, D2; tel: 01 677 9290; www. thepalacebardublin.com), a former favourite of Brendan Behan, Flann O'Brien, Patrick Kavanagh and other literary giants, and one of several city pubs still with its original Victorian interior.

Another pub worth seeking out is **Grogan's** (15 William Street South, D2; www.groganspub.ie). Small, scruffy and old-fashioned, it draws an eclectic crowd of all ages.

NIGHTCLUBS

The greatest density of clubs is in the Temple Bar area. The **Turk's Head** (27 Parliament Street, Temple Bar, D2; www.paramounthotel.ie) is a lively club beneath the eponymous pub playing popular sounds and chart hits to a young trendy crowd, while the hugely popular bi-level **Rí-Rá**, meaning "uproar" (Dame Court, D2; www.riraclub.ie), plays various sounds – funk, house, garage, pop, soul – on different nights of the week.

Club M (Cope Street, Temple Bar, D2; www.clubm.ie) is one of the larger nightclubs featuring dance, R 'n' B and chart; it's a mainstream venue (yes, chrome is present) but pleases most people most of the time. It has a couple of large chill-out areas and there are laser shows that provide dramatic effect. As the club is spread out over two floors, there are also some separate VIP areas that are available for exclusive use with advance booking. Overall, the club tends to attract visitors under 30.

LIVE MUSIC VENUES

Dublin has had a thriving rock scene ever since local band Thin Lizzy made it big in the 1970s, and this part of the city embraces some of the most popular live music venues. Among them, atmospheric **Whelan's** (25 Wexford Street, D2; www.whelanslive.com) is a long-standing gig venue specializing in rock, jazz and traditional music, and featuring the best new Irish bands nightly and an after-hours club at the weekend.

The Button Factory (Curved Street, D2; www.buttonfactory.ie) once the Temple Bar Music Centre, is one of Dublin's most exciting multi-purpose venues. Bands, DJs and other acts benefit from a state-of-the-art sound system. Acts and events scheduled daily range from hip indie bands to world music, and from Thursday to Saturday there's an "after-hours" club.

Temple Bar is the setting for live Irish music of varying quality; try going to midweek sessions

Southside West

rather than fight through the inebriated crowds at weekends.

The following pubs all offer live music ranging from fiddle sessions to jazz and rock: the **Auld Dubliner** (24–25 Temple Bar, D2; tel: 01 677 0527; www.aulddubliner.ie), an old-style bar with live music every night and known for its local and foreign bands; the **Temple Bar** (47–48 Temple Bar, D2; www.thetemplebarpub.com), with Irish music, garden and fine collection of whiskeys; The Oliver St John Gogarty (58–59 Fleet Street, D2; www.gogartys.ie), which offers a daily dose of traditional music on the first floor as well as above-average Irish food (including Irish stew, Galway prawns and beef and Guinness casserole); the **Porterhouse** (16 Parliament Street, D2; www.theporterhouse.ie), a buzzy, multi-level pub with nightly live music and home-brewed beers; and the **Viper Room** (5 Aston Quay, D2; tel: 01 672 5566), another lively pub which has a late-night upstairs jazz bar.

Another possibility is the **Vat House Bar** (www.vathouse.ie) in Blooms Hotel on Anglesea Street in Temple Bar, which has live Irish music every night.

West along the Liffey, the **Brazen Head** (Bridge Street, D8; www.brazenhead.com) proudly proclaims itself Dublin's oldest pub, although there's not really that much left of the 12th-century building. Its Sunday afternoon sessions are extremely popular, with a band ready to play for anyone who fancies stretching their vocal chords. It also provides traditional Irish food, such as Irish stew, oysters and Guinness.

Further west, **Vicar Street** (58–59 Thomas Street, D8; www.vicarstreet.com) is one of Dublin's stalwart live venues for both music and stand-up comedy, offering a regular programme of renowned names and even the occasional legend.

CLASSICAL MUSIC

Lovers of choral music should take the opportunity to hear the male choristers at **St Patrick's Cathedral** (➤ 65) during daily Evensong. The cathedral also holds occasional concerts by visiting choirs and annual performances of Handel's *Messiah*.

Christ Church Cathedral (➤ 76) also presents concerts by visiting choirs as well as its own mixed adult and girls' choirs. Before services on Sunday, listen out for Christ Church's famous bell ringing; on New Year's Eve, thousands gather outside the cathedral to hear the bells ring in the New Year.

THEATRE & CINEMA

The **Olympia Theatre** (72 Dame Street, D2; www.olympia.ie) has the feel of a Victorian music hall and presents an eclectic range of productions, from popular musicals to stand-up. It occasionally also attracts Irish folk bands, and rock and pop artists. Most Fridays and Saturdays, around midnight, the theatre is transformed into a lively late-night music venue with upbeat live music acts.

In Temple Bar, the **Project Arts Centre** (39 Essex Street East, Temple Bar, D2; www.projectartscentre.ie) offers a multi-disciplinary programme with experimental theatre, dance, Live Art and film.

Further west, **Tivoli Theatre** (135–138 Francis Street, D8; www.tivoli.ie) is located in a converted cinema and presents a range of entertainment, from Shakespeare to pantomime and live big jazz bands.

Film buffs should head to the **Irish Film Institute** (6 Eustace Street, Temple Bar, D2; tel: 01 679 5744; www.ifi.ie), which shows mostly independent, art-house and foreign films. During the summer Temple Bar's Meeting House Square is turned into an open-air cinema with evening screenings of classic films.

Insider Tip

Southside East

 **Little Treats**

Lunch in an Art Gallery
Enjoy a delicious meal in the **National Gallery's** (➤101) bright self-service cafe, where the free water is available in jugs on the tables.

Sophisticated Pleasure
It's hard to imagine a more beautiful setting to indulge in an opulent Afternoon Tea than the Lord Mayor's Lounge in the **Shelbourne Hotel** (➤116).

One-on-one with Louise Kennedy
The Irish fashion designer's boutique is housed over five floors of a town house on **Merrion Square** (➤111; tel: 01 662 0056) where visits are by appointment only.

Getting Your Bearings

Southside East is bursting with the colours, sights and scenes that encapsulate the very essence of the city centre. Just south of the Liffey, this has been Dublin's most elegant and fashionable area for centuries. Here you can marvel at the treasures contained within the cluster of museums, including the National Gallery and the National Museum; wander along the Grand Canal; enjoy the buzz of Grafton Street at the epicentre of the main shopping district; relax in quiet, secluded leafy parks; lap up the atmosphere at one of the neighbourhood's chic outdoor cafes or its traditional pubs; and experience the peacefulness of Trinity College right in the heart of the bustling city…and what's more, everything is within a few minutes' walk of each other.

This area also marks the epitome of Dublin's glorious Georgian era (1714–1830), best seen in the wide streets and the finely preserved squares and terraces that today form the main business sector of the capital. Of the several thousand Georgian houses in Dublin, no two doors are the same. Each has elaborately decorated fanlights, side windows, door knobs and knockers. The triumph of the Georgian terrace is each house's individuality, contained within a prescribed uniformity, all based on the designs of classical antiquity. Indeed, it is these minute touches of personality – the ornate wrought-iron balconies, coal-hole covers and boot-scrapers – which are the rewards of a sharp-eyed visitor to this district.

TOP 10

At Your Leisure

Getting Your Bearings

The splendid National Museum of Ireland – Archaeology on Kildare Street

Custom House

Tara St Station

River Liffey

City Quay

Aston Quay

Townsend Street

Wax Plus

Bank of Ireland **22** **23**

College St

Pearse St

Sandwith St Lower

Trinity College

Book of Kells

College Park

Pearse Station

Wicklow St

Nassau St

Lincoln Pl

Westland Row

Fenian St

Duke St

Grafton Street **24**

Anne St South

Dawson St

National Library of Ireland **26**

St Ann's Church **25**

Kildare St

National Gallery of Ireland

27 Leinster House

Merrion Square North

St South

National Museum of Ireland – Archaeology

28

National Museum of Ireland – Natural History

29 Merrion Square

Merrion Square South

St Stephen's Green West

St Stephen's Green North

St Stephen's Green

St Stephen's Green East

10 St Stephen's Green

Merrion Row

30 Number Twenty Nine

St Stephen's Green South

Leeson St Lower

Pembroke St Lower

Fitzwilliam Lower

Iveagh Gardens

Fitz-william Sq.

Imaginosity **31**

0   200 m
0   200 yd

The Perfect Day

If you're not quite sure where to begin your travels, this itinerary recommends a practical and enjoyable day in Southside East, taking in some of the best places to see. For more information see the main entries (➤ 92–112).

🕘 9:00am

Start your day exploring the picturesque cobbled quadrangles and ancient playing fields of ⭐**Trinity College** (right; ➤ 92). Head to the Old Library to see one of the city's greatest treasures – the magnificent eighth-century Celtic-Christian manuscript, the ⭐*Book of Kells* (➤ 96) – renowned as the most beautiful book in the world. Adjacent to the *Book of Kells* display is the splendid Long Room, containing the college's historic library.

🕚 11:00am

After coffee and a cake in **Avoca Café** (➤ 113), head to Grafton Street, the spine of Dublin's main shopping district, and watch the buyers go by. Then cut down Anne Street South and along Molesworth Street to the ⭐**National Museum of Ireland – Archaeology** (➤ 98) to view the dazzling collection of prehistoric gold and jewels, including the Ardagh Chalice. Alternatively, visit the ⭐**National Gallery of Ireland** (➤ 101), around the corner on Merrion Square, with its excellent Irish and European collections.

🕧 12:30pm

Enjoy a relaxing lunch in one of the classy town-house restaurants on 🔟**St Stephen's Green** (left; ➤ 104). Try Thornton's for Modern Irish cuisine, or **Shanahan's** (➤ 116), an up-market steakhouse. Alternatively get a takeaway from one of the sandwich bars and join the locals and the ducks in the park.

Perfect Days in...

🕐 **2:00pm**

You now have plenty of time to explore Georgian Dublin. **29 Merrion Square** (► 111), neighbouring Fitzwilliam Square and the streets in between form its heart, with their beguilingly elegant symmetry. Even though the vast majority of houses are now occupied as offices, it is not too hard to wind the clock back, especially on the quieter streets, and imagine you are back in a more refined era.

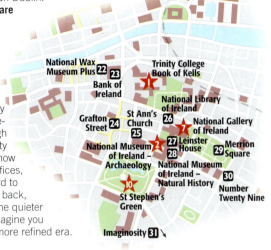

National Wax Museum Plus 22 23
Bank of Ireland
Trinity College Book of Kells
National Library of Ireland
Grafton Street 24
St Ann's Church 25
National Gallery of Ireland 26 7
National Museum of Ireland – Archaeology 2 27 Leinster House 28
Merrion Square 29
National Museum of Ireland – Natural History
Number Twenty Nine 30
St Stephen's Green 10
Imaginosity 31

🕐 **3:30pm**

Return to **24 Grafton Street** (below; ► 109) to browse or shop in the luxury boutiques that flank Dublin's famous shop-till-you-drop thoroughfare. Then join other shoppers relaxing in the Lord Mayor's Lounge at **The Shelbourne Hotel** (► 116) – the perfect spot for a sedate afternoon tea with sandwiches, home-made pastries and scones with jam and cream.

🕐 **7:00pm**

Go on the Literary Pub Crawl (► 171), starting in the **Duke** (9 Duke Street) just off Grafton Street. Actors on the tour perform scenes from works by James Joyce, Brendan Behan, George Bernard Shaw, Oscar Wilde and others, between leading you into various pubs for a pint or two.

🕐 **9:30pm**

With the tour over, the night is yours. Why not continue pubbing? After all, you have over a thousand watering-holes to choose from in the city, so enjoy a night of mighty good *craic*!

⭐ Trinity College & the *Book of Kells*

Entering the peaceful grounds of Ireland's oldest and most famous university, with its glorious cluster of 18th-century buildings, lawns and cobbled quadrangles, is like stepping into a world far removed from the hustle and bustle of the city that surrounds it. Apart from a star-studded list of alumni, including most of the giants of Irish literature, Trinity is best known today as the home of the priceless *Book of Kells*, the greatest Celtic illuminated gospel in existence, considered by many to be the most beautiful book in the world.

Trinity College

Queen Elizabeth I founded Trinity College in 1592 on the site of an Augustinian monastery – at that time the college grounds were outside the original walled city. It was during her reign that Ireland developed into a British colony, and her aim in creating Trinity College was "for the reformation of the barbarism of this rude people…to civilize Ireland through learning and to cure them of their Popery by establishing a true religion within the realm." Thus Trinity became a seat of Protestant learning. After 1873, Catholics were officially allowed to become students but, up until 1966, they had to obtain a special dispensation to attend

Parliament Square at Trinity College

on pain of excommunication. It is only in the past few decades that they have joined in any significant number and of the 8,000 students in attendance today around 70 per cent are Catholic.

At 17ha (42 acres), Trinity College is also one of Ireland's largest universities. Although nothing remains of the original buildings, the campus contains a unique collection of magnificent 18th-century halls. The main entrance is on College Green (opposite the Bank of Ireland, ➤ 108), a busy road intersection where 400 years ago Dubliners grazed their cattle, and where public executions were staged. Two statues of famous graduates flank the entrance: the political essayist and statesman Edmund Burke (to the left) and writer Oliver Goldsmith (to the right). The elegant, colonnaded facade hardly deserves Joyce's harsh description, "a surly front, a dull stone set in the ring of the city's ignorance", but rather it sets the tone for the grand ensemble of buildings within.

CELEBRITY STUDENTS

Illustrious past students here include writers Jonathan Swift, Oliver Goldsmith, Oscar Wilde, John Millington Synge, Bram Stoker and Samuel Beckett; patriots and politicians Theobald Wolfe Tone, Robert Emmet, Edward Carson, Henry Grattan and Thomas Davis; philosophers George Berkeley and Edmund Burke; Ireland's first president, Douglas Hyde, and one of its most recent, Mary Robinson.

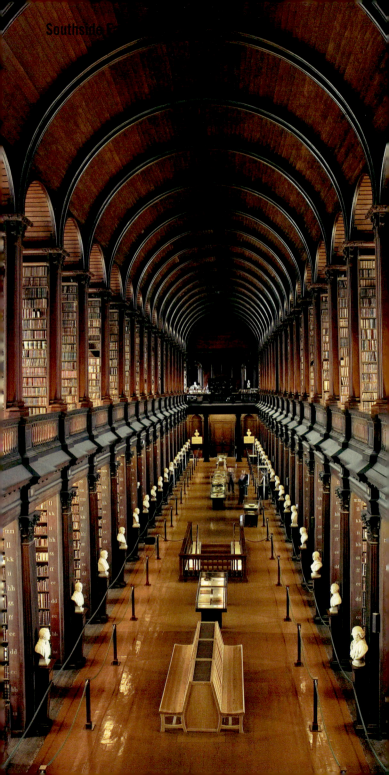

Statues of Oliver Goldsmith (above) and Edmund Burke (above right) at the university entrance

Left: The splendid Long Room

On entering the college into the first quadrangle, **Parliament Square**, there is an immediate collegiate atmosphere – a sense of tranquillity and ancient seclusion. On the left, the chapel is the only church in the Republic shared by all the Christian denominations. The formal classicism of the chapel is almost mirrored on the opposite side of the square by the Examination Hall, with its noble portico, ornate ceilings and a magnificent gilded oak chandelier that originally hung in the old Irish Parliament. Both buildings, designed by William Chambers and dating from the late 18th century, are set off by atmospheric cobbles, antique lamps and cast-iron bollards.

Straight ahead of you is the most photographed feature of Trinity – a 30m (100-ft) **campanile**, donated in 1853 by Lord Beresford, the Archbishop of Armagh, which tolls every summer to summon students to their examinations. Beyond the bell tower, the row of red-brick buildings (known as the Rubrics) with their unusual gabled architecture is the oldest surviving part of the college. Today it is a hall of residence. Pity the undergraduate living in No 25 – it is said to be haunted by an unpopular tutor who was shot by an anonymous student.

Beside the Rubrics, to the right, is the **Old Library**. Bear round the end of the building into Fellows' Square, a grassy quadrangle flanked by mostly modern buildings, including the **Douglas Hyde Art Gallery**, which presents an annual series of carefully selected exhibitions by undiscovered or marginalized artists.

SAMUEL BECKETT (1906–89)

Nobel Prize-winner and modern Irish playwright Samuel Beckett was born in Foxrock, a southern suburb of Dublin. Like his fellow Irish writers George Bernard Shaw, Oscar Wilde and WB Yeats, he came from a Protestant, Anglo-Irish background. From 1923 to 1927 he studied Romance languages at Trinity College, where he received his bachelor's degree. He was also a keen member of the college cricket team. During the early 1930s he moved to Paris where he wrote many of his greatest works, including *Waiting for Godot*, *More Pricks Than Kicks*, *Krapp's Last Tape* and *Endgame*. Today the Samuel Beckett Theatre – part of the drama department on the Pearse Street side of the campus – stands in testimony to Trinity's great alumnus.

Southside East

The entrance to the Old Library, the complex's earliest surviving building, is via the bookshop on your left. Here you will find Trinity's most precious treasure, the *Book of Kells*, and the splendid Long Room (left) containing the historic university library.

The *Book of Kells*

Although surprisingly small, the Book of Kells is undoubtedly one of the finest manuscripts to survive from the first Christian millennium. It contains a lavishly decorated transcription, in Latin, of the four gospels, inscribed on vellum parchment and intricately ornamented with colourful patterns, human figures and exotic, fanciful animals. It was discovered in the town of Kells near Newgrange (➤ 152) in County Meath, but it was probably written by four Irish missionary monks on the island of Iona, off the west coast of Scotland, around AD800. It is thought they fled to Kells in AD806 after a Viking raid, and completed the book there. The Irish Church at this time was largely monastic in organization and the message of the life of Christ was spread primarily through gospel books; the scribes and artists who produced them held an honoured place in Irish society. The book was sent to Dublin around 1653 for security reasons during the Cromwellian period.

The grand main entrance through the Front Gate at night

Two other manuscripts are also selected for display from the books of *Durrow*, *Armagh*, *Dimma* and *Mulling*, each as old as the *Book of Kells*. They lie in a glass case at the end of an excellent exhibition entitled Turning Darkness into Light, which places the *Book of Kells* (and the other manuscripts) in its historical and cultural context. It also enables the visitor to view sections of the manuscript in much greater detail than would otherwise be possible, and to study the techniques used by the scribes, the colours (chalk for white, lead for red, lapis lazuli for blue, carbon for black and copper verdigris for green), the inspirations for their designs, the various symbols and the recurring imagery.

Trinity College & the *Book of Kells*

The more you look at them, the more you see: sinners misbehaving, symbols of Christ (lions, snakes, fish and peacocks), angels, floral tendrils, and conundrums of geometry that resolve, as you stare at them, into elaborate initial letters.

The Long Room

Leading on from the *Book of Kells* display, the 18th-century Long Room, with its hushed air and high barrel-vaulted oak ceiling of cathedral proportions, contains more than 200,000 of Ireland's most important antiquarian books, manuscripts and historical documents, together with 48 white marble busts of noteworthy scholars, including Jonathan Swift. This grandiose hall, 66m (220ft) in length and 12m (40ft) in height, contains a double-decker layer of dark wood floor-to-ceiling shelving in 20 arched bays, with leather-bound books, ladders and beautifully carved spiral staircases. With its stock of nearly 3 million volumes, it is widely regarded as one of the great research libraries of the world. Also in the Long Room is one of the handful of remaining copies of the 1916 Proclamation of the Irish, which signalled the start of the Easter Rising when it was read aloud by Pádraic Pearse outside the General Post Office on 24 April 1916 (➤ 131). It's displayed to one side as you enter.

TAKING A BREAK

Check out **Kilkenny Shop's** (➤ 115) self-service restaurant overlooking the grounds of Trinity College or one of several branches of Leon in the vicinity.

✚ 191 F3 ✉ College Green, D2 (other entrances on Nassau Street and Leinster Street South) ☎ 01 896 2320
🕙 The campus is open to visitors seven days a week
🚌 All cross-city buses 🚃 DART: Tara Street

The Old Library & the *Book of Kells*
☎ www.tcd.ie 🕙 Mon–Sat 9:30–5, and Sun 9:30–4:30 (May–Sep); Sun noon–4:30 (Oct–Apr) 💶 €10

Douglas Hyde Gallery
☎ 01 896 1116; www.douglashydegallery.com
🕙 Mon–Fri 11–6 (to 7 Thu), Sat 11–4:45 💶 Free

INSIDER INFO

- **Arrive early** to avoid the crowds to see the famed *Book of Kells*, or visit out of season when there are fewer visitors.
- Tours of the College campus include entry to see the *Book of Kells*.
- Ireland's oldest surviving **harp**, dating from the 15th century, upon which the harp emblem found on Irish coinage is based, can be seen in the Long Room.
- Lively, informative **walking tours** of the college take place every 25 minutes during the summer months from Front Square. Ask at the porter's desk for information.

Insider Tip

★2 National Museum of Ireland – Archaeology

Not only does the National Museum in Kildare Street contain Ireland's most treasured antiquities, it brings to life the country's rich heritage and unique history from 7000BC to the start of Irish Independence in 1921 through its magnificent collections, which include some outstanding examples of Celtic and medieval art and one of the world's largest and finest collections of prehistoric gold.

On arrival, notice ==the entrance hall – a dazzling domed rotunda with columns made of Irish marble and a mosaic floor depicting signs of the zodiac.== **Insider Tip**

The first collection on the ground floor, **Prehistoric Ireland**, transports visitors back to the Stone Age, with its flints, vessels, tools, weapons and domestic objects, some dating from as early as 7000BC. The huge Lurgan logboat – Ireland's earliest surviving boat (*c.* 2500BC), hewn out of an oak trunk – is a particular highlight, together with a reconstructed neolithic passage tomb and a remarkably intact body of a man who lay for centuries beneath a

Priceless treasures fill the museum's main gallery

**Left from top:
The prized
Ardagh Chalice;
c. 800–700BC
gold collar; the
eighth-century
Tara Brooch**

Galway bog before being transported to the capital with fragments of his leather cloak.

Many important pieces in the museum were dug by chance from peat bogs that have natural preservative qualities enabling objects of metal, fabric and wood to survive in good condition for thousands of years.

The exhibits lead you chronologically through the major changes and developments of the period, and provide a context for **Ór – Ireland's Gold**, the breathtaking exhibition of prehistoric gold in the centre of the exhibition hall. The gleaming gold jewellery dating from the Bronze Age (c. 2000–700BC) is particularly noteworthy, with its ornamental necklaces, beads, bangles, dress fasteners, its finely beaten *lunulae* (crescent-shaped collars) and *torcs* (twisted necklaces and waistbands). Even today, these styles are frequently copied by modern jewellery makers.

The greatest treasures of Celtic and Irish medieval art are displayed in the **Treasury**, to the right of the prehistoric collections, in particular the Ardagh Chalice, the Cross of Cong and the Tara Brooch. The eighth-century **Ardagh**

Southside East

Chalice, a heavily decorated, twin-handled silver cup, was found by a labourer named Quinn while digging up potatoes near Ardagh in County Limerick. Unaware of its true value, he sold his "treasure" to a local doctor for just a few pounds. The intricate processional **Cross of Cong**, with its beaded silver wire, decorative animal heads and inlaid enamel work, was made in 1123 for Turlough O'Conor, King of Connacht, to contain a relic of the True Cross. The eighth-century **Tara Brooch**, with its delicate copper designs set against a silver background, studded with amber and coloured glass, bird and animal ornamentation and thistle motifs, represents the summit of Irish jewellery. You can also see smaller personal items and collections of silver coins.

Upstairs, you can experience Dublin life during the 🧒 **Viking Age** (AD795–1170), with a vast range of fascinating items ranging from pots and pans, gaming boards, jewellery, toys, shoes, even Viking graffiti, dug up in the Christ Church/Wood Quay area of town.

Also on the upper floor are the **Medieval Ireland** galleries with exhibits relating to Power, Work and Prayer from 1150 to 1550. The galleries show the lives of nobles, peasants and the clergy, illustrating the importance of agriculture, weapons and religion to society.

The **Kingship and Sacrifice** exhibition sheds light on the Iron Age "bog bodies" that have been unearthed in Ireland. The items displayed include royal regalia, weapons and utensils used for feasts.

The museum also holds finds from Egypt and Ancient Cyprus as well as a range of items from Roman times, collected from around the world.

TAKING A BREAK

The museum's cafe serves tasty snacks, salads, sandwiches and pastries. Alternatively, try **Kilkenny** (► 115) close by.

➕ 185 D3 ✉ Kildare Street, D2
☎ 01 677 7444; www.museum.ie
🕐 Tue–Sat 10–5, Sun 2–5
🚌 25, 33, 41, 51, 66, 67, 84 🚆 DART: Pearse Street

⭐ National Gallery of Ireland

The gallery houses Ireland's foremost collection of Irish and Old Master paintings. More than 700 paintings are on display with representative works from all the major schools of European painting, as well as the remarkable national collection of Irish art from the late 17th century onwards.

The National Gallery was established by an Act of Parliament in 1854 and erected as a public testimonial to William Dargan, the designer of Ireland's railways and organizer of the Dublin Exhibition of 1853, a massive showcase of Irish craft and industry that took place in a temporary structure on the adjoining Leinster Lawn. Many of the paintings in that exhibition formed the nucleus of the early collection. The event inspired the assembly of works of art on a more permanent basis, to serve as an inspiration for up-and-coming Irish artists, and the gallery was opened to the public in 1864, with just 125 paintings. A statue of William Dargan, unveiled at the inauguration, stands outside the gallery.

The opening of an award-winning Millennium Wing in 2002 has greatly increased the size of the gallery and, since its foundation, the stature of the collection has grown considerably. Today it boasts some 2,500 paintings

The Dargan Wing

Southside East

and approximately 10,000 other works in different media, including watercolour, drawing, print and sculpture.

In addition to the national collection of European Old Masters, the gallery's main emphasis is on its exceptional array of Irish paintings (the majority of which are on permanent display), and the **Yeats Museum**, opened in March 1999 by the then Taoiseach, Bertie Ahern. The museum is dedicated to the work of 20th-century Irish painter Jack Butler Yeats and his family. Look out for *The Liffey Swim* and other Dublin cityscapes.

The European collections (Spanish, Flemish, Dutch, French and Italian schools) are on the second floor. Picasso's *Still Life with Mandolin*; Vermeer's *Lady Writing a Letter, with her Maid* and Velázquez's *Supper at Emmaus* count among the most celebrated European paintings, together with Caravaggio's *The Taking of Christ*, a veritable masterpiece, found by chance in a Dublin Jesuit's house in 1990, which has since greatly enhanced the gallery's international reputation.

The Beit Wing of the National Gallery

Spiral staircase inside the gallery

The gallery's 19th-century facade illuminated at night

TAKING A BREAK

Treat yourself to a light lunch of traditional Irish fare at the popular wine bar **Ely** (➤ 114), just a stone's throw from the gallery in Ely Place, or enjoy a light bite in the gallery's cafe.

✚ 192 B2
✉ Merrion Square West and Clare Street, D2
☎ 01 661 5133; www.nationalgallery.ie
🕐 Mon–Sat 9:30–5:30 (Thu to 8:30), Sun 11–5:30. Guided tours Sat 12:30, Sun 12:30 and 1:30, extra tours Jul, Aug – ask at information desk
🚌 4, 7, 8, 39A, 46A 🚉 DART: Pearse Street 💷 Free

INSIDER INFO

Here's how to get the best out of a visit to the National Gallery.

- The best introduction to the paintings is to attend one of the free **lectures or guided tours**. Pick up a copy of the small magazine *Gallery News* for up-to-date details.
- The gallery also organizes 👫 **family activity programmes** (Sat at 3pm) and, during school holidays, special "Little Masters" Discovery Club for children and workshops for various age groups.
- **Free audio guide** to permanent collection, available in six languages. Also available free for hire is a 👫 children's audio guide to the permanent collection for ages 6–13 years.
- Don't miss the **Impressionist Collection**, with works by Monet, Degas, Pissarro, Sisley, Van Gogh, Bonnard and others.
- **Amorino**, a marble statue of Cupid by Italian sculptor Antonio Canova.

Insider Tip

⭐10 St Stephen's Green

This lush oasis of tranquillity right at the heart of the city, commonly called "The Green", provides welcome respite from the congestion of urban life and is a natural antidote to its noise, streets and pollution. Beloved for its duck pond, statues and free lunchtime concerts in summer, on warm, sunny days the park is filled with office workers, families and visitors sitting, strolling, picnicking and relaxing on the grass. No wonder James Joyce called it "the soul of the city".

The Green was originally a piece of common grazing ground. It was close to a leper colony and used for public hangings. Building round the square began in 1663, when wealthy citizens could construct a house only if they planted six healthy sycamore trees on the Green. Before long, it became a private residents' square, and by the latter half of the 18th century it was *the* place for the aristocracy to promenade in their finery.

The four sides, each nearly 500m in length, had their own named "walks", the most sought after being the "Beaux Walk" on the north side, which to this day remains the most fashionable, overlooked by the exclusive Shelbourne Hotel (➤ 46).

St Stephen's Green was converted into a public park in 1880 by Arthur Edward Guinness, the owner of the Guinness Brewery, who later became Lord Ardilaun. Today this 9ha (22-acre) "National Historic Park" holds a special place in

Lazy summer days relaxing in the park

Dubliners' hearts, with its manicured lawns, formal Victorian flower displays, picturesque paved walks, ponds, fountains and bandstand, not to mention the memorials to many of the city's famous citizens.

Right: The Wolfe Tone Memorial

Memorials
The park's main memorials are located at the corner entrances. The **Fusilier's Arch**, resembling a Roman triumphal arch at the Grafton Street entrance, commemorates the Royal Dublin Fusiliers lost in the Second Boer War in South Africa.

The **Three Fates Fountain** at the Leeson Street entrance was a gift from the German people in thanks for Irish help to refugees in the aftermath of World War II, while the modern memorial near Merrion Row to the "Father" of Irish republican nationalism, Theobald Wolfe Tone (▶ 21), is better known as **"Tonehenge"**.

Notable Buildings
Although St Stephen's Green is one of the landmarks of Georgian Dublin, there was no overall plan to the buildings and the Green is notable for the variety in age and style of

Southside East

its houses. The finest Georgian buildings include the Royal College of Surgeons on the west side and Newman House to the south.

The internationally renowned **Royal College of Surgeons**, with more than a thousand students from all over the world, was designed by Edward Parke in 1806 and is one of the jewels in the city's Georgian crown, with its granite-faced, neoclassical facade and distinctive round-headed windows. The three statues atop the pediment are Hygieia (goddess of health), Asclepius (god of medicine) and Athena (goddess of wisdom). The building played an important part in the 1916 Easter Rising, when it was occupied by rebel troops under the feisty Countess Markievicz (▶ 22), and you can still see some bullet scars on the facade.

The two restored Georgian town houses comprising **Newman House** (Nos 85–86) contain some of Ireland's most ornate 18th-century plasterwork. Look in particular in the Bishops' Room, Hopkins' Study and the Apollo Room, with its magnificent Apollo, his nine muses and countless cherubs. In 1865, the buildings became part of the first Roman Catholic university allowed in the city after the Restoration, although ironically No 86 was originally built for the vehement anti-Catholic politician Thomas "Burnchapel" Whaley. Cardinal Newman was the first rector, and the crouching lion on the facade has observed the comings and goings of such notable students as writers James Joyce and Flann O'Brien; two leading figures in the 1916 uprising, Pádraic Pearse and Éamon de Valera; and the celebrated poet and priest Gerard Manley Hopkins, professor of classics here from 1884 to 1889.

Beside Newman House, the **University Church** looks nothing from the outside, but inside it is a gem of neo-Byzantine splendour, popular with students for marriage ceremonies. Nearby **Iveagh House** was donated to the state by Rupert Guinness, Second Earl of Iveagh, in 1939. Its interior, housing the Department of Foreign Affairs, is one of the

The neo-Byzantine interior of University Church

The historic Shelbourne Hotel

most sumptuous in all Dublin but is sadly closed to the public. Hidden beyond Iveagh House is the lovely, secluded secret park of little-known **Iveagh Gardens** (➤ 34).

The most prominent building on the Green is **The Shelbourne Hotel** (➤ 46), a venerable Dublin institution immortalized in James Joyce's *Ulysses*, and the traditional place for old-fashioned afternoon tea after the day's shopping is done. For almost two centuries it has opened its doors to the famous, the influential and the notorious, hosting everyone from royalty to rock stars. History has unfolded within its walls: the British garrisoned the hotel during the 1916 Rising and the Free State Constitution was drafted here in 1922. But such was the importance attached to providing impeccable service at the Shelbourne that, even when the Easter Rising broke out, afternoon tea wasn't cancelled. It was simply moved to the Writing Room!

■ TAKING A BREAK

Take your pick from the numerous stylish restaurants fringing the Green – **La Mere Zou** (➤ 115) is particularly good value for lunch – or buy provisions and have a picnic on the Green.

🕂 191 E1 ℹ️ www.ststephensgreenpark.ie
🕐 Mon–Sat at 7:30, Sun and hols at 9:30. The gates are locked at dusk
🚌 7, 11, 25, 33, 37, 38, 46A, 8 🚇 LUAS: St Stephen's Green

Newman House
🕂 191 E1 ☎ 01 716 7422 🕐 Jun–Aug Tue–Fri (tours at 2, 3, 4) 💶 €5

At Your Leisure

22 🚻 National Wax Museum Plus

Dublin's answer to Madame Tussauds is huge fun, especially for children. The main part of the museum concentrates on the people and events that shaped Ireland's history, with life-sized figures of such luminaries as Robert Emmet, James Joyce and the Taoiseach, while the Hall of the Megastars focuses on the world of pop, including U2. Also popular is the Chamber of Horrors. ==For younger children there are puppet shows four times daily.== **Insider Tip**

➕ 191 D3 ✉ 4 Foster Place, Temple Bar
☎ 01 671 8373; www.waxmuseumplus.ie
🕐 Daily 10–7 💶 €12, children €8

23 Bank of Ireland (Parliament House)

The curving Palladian facade of the Bank of Ireland marks one of Dublin's most striking buildings. Originally designed by Edward Lovett Pearce in 1729 to house the Irish Parliament, it was the first

Bank of Ireland facade

purpose-built parliament in the world containing a two-chamber legislature. For more than half a century Irish affairs of State were governed from here, and within its walls in 1782 the Independence of the Irish Nation was declared. However, the building became redundant when, in 1800, the Irish Parliament was cajoled and bribed into voting through the Act of Union, shifting direct rule from Dublin to London, and thereby voting itself out of existence.

The Bank of Ireland purchased Parliament House in 1802 for IR£40,000. During banking hours you can visit the House of Lords, with its original barrel-vaulted ceiling, oak and marble fireplace, glittering Waterford chandelier and massive tapestries. The British Government insisted that all traces of the House of Commons were removed, but the mace, made in 1765, has been preserved and can be seen in the House of Lords room. This is open during banking hours; tours explain the background.

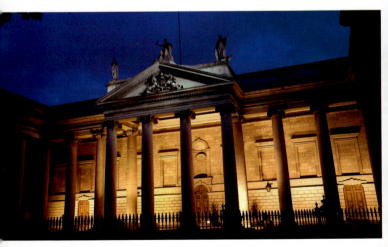

Musicians in Grafton Street

🏛 191 E3 ✉ College Green, D2
☎ 01 661 5933 🕐 House of Lords: Mon–Fri
10–4, Thu till 5; guided tours Mon–Fri 10:30,
11:30, 1:30 🚌 All city-centre buses 💶 Free

24 Grafton Street

Grafton Street is immortalized
in many a song and story, and
is a "must see" for any visitor.
Pedestrianized and crowded from
morning till night, there's always
an electric atmosphere here. The
many street entertainers draw
crowds outside the high-street
stores and exclusive boutiques
and there are plenty of tempting
cafes and snug Irish pubs.
🏛 191 E2 ✉ Grafton Street, D2
🚌 All city-centre buses

25 St Ann's Church

The best view of St Ann's Church
is from Grafton Street, looking
down Anne Street South at its
striking neo-Romanesque facade.
The church was created in 1707
for the rapidly evolving Georgian
suburbs, with private pews for
distinguished residents such as
the Duke of Leinster, the archbishop and the lord mayor. The
18th-century nationalist leader
Theobald Wolfe Tone married
here in 1785, as did Bram Stoker,
author of *Dracula*, in 1878.
Dublin-born philanthropist Thomas
Barnardo attended Sunday school
here as a boy, before opening a
boys' home in London's East End
slums in 1869, which marked the
start of a vast organisation for
homeless children known as
Barnardo's Homes.

St Ann's also has a long tradition
of charity work. In 1723 Baron
Butler left a bequest to
provide 120 loaves
of bread each week
for the poor. To this
day any person may
take a loaf from the
shelf situated just
beside the altar.
🏛 191 E2
✉ Dawson Street, D2
☎ 01 676 7727;
www.stann.dublin.anglican.org
🕐 Mon–Fri 10–4
🚌 All city-centre buses
💶 Free

tional Wax
useum Plus   Bank of
        22   Ireland   College St
             23   Pearse St
                    Trinity College
                    ★
                    Book of Kells
        Nassau   St
    Grafton
    Street 24   St Ann's
                  25 Church Kildare St
                 Dawson St

Southside East

26 National Library of Ireland

The National Library was opened in 1890 to house the collection of the Royal Dublin Society. From the start it has endeavoured to collect all material of Irish interest or of Irish origin published in the world, and holds some 5 million items on 11km (7mi) of shelves and in its vast archives. It also administers the **Genealogical Office**, designing and granting coats of arms, and helping anyone with an Irish background find out about their ancestors. You need to sign a visitor's book to get inside the main section of the National Library. **Insider Tip**

Its *pièce de résistance*, however, is the wonderful domed Reading Room with its narrow arched windows separated by pilasters that appear to lean inwards. The space is especially atmospheric on a gloomy winter's evening, with each desk lit by a green, glowing reading lamp and the impressive dome overhead like a giant, encouraging brain.

In 2002, the National Library acquired a remarkable collection of James Joyce manuscripts, consisting mainly of previously unknown

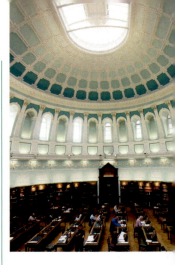

The domed Reading Room in the National Library

drafts of *Ulysses*. Together with other material on Joyce's work and life, the manuscripts are now on display in a semi-permanent exhibition at the library, providing a fascinating background to his ground-breaking novel (➤ 136).

🕂 192 B2 ✉ Kildare Street, D2
☎ 01 603 0200; www.nli.ie
🕐 Mon–Wed 9:30–8, Thu, Fri till 5, Sat till 1
🚌 7B, 7D, 11, 39A, 46A, 116, 118, 145
🚉 DART: Pearse Street 💷 Free

27 Leinster House

Leinster House is arguably Dublin's finest Georgian town house. When, in 1745, the Earl of Kildare built Kildare House on a green-field site south of Trinity College, many others followed his example, hence the many Georgian avenues and squares of the neighbourhood.

The house was renamed after the Earl became Duke of Leinster in 1766. It was the largest Georgian town house in Ireland. The Duke reputedly never liked it, nor could he agree with his architect, Richard Castle, on which side should be the front, so both sides were decided upon: the Kildare Street facade has the appearance of a large, ornate town house, while the Merrion Square facade resembles a country

---

OFF THE BEATEN TRACK

Anyone checking out the city's musical landmarks is sure to visit **Windmill Lane** (off Sir John Rogerson's Quay), where the band U2 made their first album at Windmill recording studios. Its walls are a spectacular sight, smothered in graffiti messages in tribute to the city's various musical heroes. Nearby, the so-called "Box on the Docks", the **Waterways Visitor Centre** (tel: 01 677 7510; www.waterwaysireland.org; Mon–Fri 10–6; entry fee €8), on the Grand Canal houses an interactive multimedia exhibition exploring Ireland's inland waterways, their historical background and their modern amenity uses. From here, it is a pleasant two-hour stroll along the Grand Canal's towpath to Kilmainham.

estate. In 1922, the house was acquired by the Irish Free State, and today houses *An Dáil Éireann* – the Irish Parliament.

⊞ 192 B1 ✉ Kildare Street, D2
☎ 01 618 3000; www.oireachtas.ie
🕐 Guided tours Mon, Fri 10:30 and 2:30 by appointment only
🚌 11, 14, 15, 25, 38, 39, 128, 145
🚆 DART: Pearse Street ♿ Free

National Library of Ireland 26
National Gallery of Ireland
27 **Leinster House**
National Museum of Ireland – Archaeology 2
28 **National Museum of Ireland – Natural History**
Kildare St
Merrion Square North
29 **Merrion Square**
Merrion Square South

28 National Museum of Ireland – Natural History

This marvellous zoological museum was inaugurated in 1857, when Dr David Livingstone delivered the opening lecture on his "African discoveries". It is among the world's finest and most comprehensive collections of stuffed animals, which are displayed in old Victorian cabinets. With more than 2 million species (of which roughly half are insects), it still has the ability to inspire wonder and amazement in young and old alike, despite its nickname – "the dead zoo".

The ground-floor Irish Room illustrates the country's astonishing variety of wildlife, while the World Animals Collection on the upper floor and galleries contains specimens from every corner of the globe, including a skeleton of a 22m (72ft) fin whale, beached in County Sligo, that is suspended from the museum's ceiling.

==A new hands-on Discovery Zone opened in 2010, allowing visitors to open drawers and inspect specimens.== **Insider Tip**

⊞ 192 B1 ✉ Merrion Street, D2
☎ 01 677 7444; www.museum.ie
🕐 Tue–Sat 10–5, Sun 2–5
🚌 11, 18, 25, 116, 118, 120, 145 ♿ Free

29 Merrion Square

Merrion Square is one of the capital's largest and most impressive Georgian squares. Its typical four-storey-over-basement terraced houses with brightly coloured doorways are in an excellent state of repair. Notice how the windows on the upper storeys get progressively shorter. Not only was this cheaper on window tax, it also created an illusion of height.

The oldest, finest houses are on the north side, including **No 1, Oscar**

Inside the Natural History Museum

Southside East

Wilde House, the childhood home of Oscar Wilde (➤ 18). Over the years, the square has been home to several other prominent Dubliners: **No 58** was the home of Daniel O'Connell; the writer Joseph Sheridan Le Fanu lived at **No 70**; and WB Yeats at **No 82**. In the northeastern corner, the **National Maternity Hospital**, founded in 1884, has a fine neo-Georgian facade. To the west is the National Gallery of Ireland (➤ 101) and Leinster House (➤ 110).

The green is one of the most attractive parks in town, far removed from its role in the 1840s as an emergency soup kitchen during the Great Famine. There are busts of Michael Collins and Henry Grattan amid the trees, as well as a flamboyant statue of Wilde opposite his home. The paths are lined with an assortment of street lamps: the city has always had a variety of street lighting and one example of each type has been placed in the square.

✚ 192 C1

Oscar Wilde House
🕐 Open all year to tours, minimum group size 25; book in advance at No 1 Merrion Square, D2
☎ 01 662 0281; www.amcd.ie
🚌 11, 18, 25, 116, 118, 120, 145
🚆 DART: Pearse Street 💳 €8

(Map showing: National Museum of Ireland – Archaeology [2], National Museum of Ireland – Natural History [28], Merrion Square [29], Merrion Square North, Merrion Square South, Number Twenty Nine [30], Imaginosity [31])

🔟 Number Twenty Nine

This magnificent town house has been perfectly restored and decorated, to provide an insight into the life of a typical middle-class family in the late Georgian era.

The first owner of Number Twenty Nine was a widow, Mrs Olivia Beatty, who bought the house in 1794 and moved in with her three children. An audio-visual show introduces Mrs Beatty and her late husband. The tour then leads through the various rooms of the house.

✚ 192 C1 ✉ 29 Fitzwilliam Street Lower, D2
☎ 01 702 6163; www.esb.ie
🕐 Tue–Sat 10–5; guided tours at 3pm
🚌 4, 7, 8, 38, 38A, 39, 39A
🚆 DART: Pearse Street 💳 €6

🔢 👫 Imaginosity

This is a bright, engaging and cleverly designed place where young children (under-10s only) can explore and learn in a hands-on environment. Children can try on costumes and arrange props and lighting in the theatre area, or burn off energy in the climbing section. Further areas allow children to paint and build, and there's also a dedicated play area for under-3s.

✚ 188 off C1 ✉ The Plaza, Beacon South Quarter, Sandyford, Dublin 18
☎ 01 217 6130; www.imaginosity.ie
🕐 Mon 1:30–5.30, Tue–Fri 9:30–5, Sat, Sun 10–6
🚆 LUAS to Stillorgan, walk to Plaza
💳 Children aged up to 1 year €2, 1–2 years €6, 3 years and over €8 (for 2 hours)

Merrion Square is lined with fine Georgian architecture

Where to…
Eat and Drink

Prices
Expect to pay for a three-course meal, excluding drinks but including VAT
€ under €30   €€ €30–€50   €€€ over €50

Avoca Café €

Avoca Handweavers, the renowned craftshop that has its flagship store in County Wicklow, has opened a large store in Dublin city centre (► 117) with a cafe on the top floor that makes an excellent and in-expensive stop for lunch. Among the options on the menu are hearty home-made soups, creative salads, freshly squeezed juices and tempting desserts. In the afternoon, stop off for tea with cream cakes.

🚌 191 E2 ✉ 11–13 Suffolk Street, D2
☎ 01 672 6019; www.avoca.ie
🕐 Mon–Fri 9:30–4:30, Sat till 5:30, Sun 11–5

Baan Thai €€

The elegant interior of this popular Thai restaurant – dark-wood panels, elaborately carved bar and framed oriental prints – creates a luxurious but comfortable atmosphere in which to enjoy well-executed Thai favourites such as red duck curry, chicken green curry and *pad thai* (fried rice noodles, usually with prawns or chicken). Its delicious tom yum soup is reputed to be the best in Dublin.

🚌 189 D3 ✉ 16 Merrion Road, D4
☎ 01 660 8833; www.baanthai.ie
🕐 Daily 5:30–11, and Wed–Fri 12:30–2:30

Bella Cuba €€

Tasty Cuban food and the sound of salsa make this lively eatery popular. Start with a rum-laced cocktail before tucking into tasty black bean soup, *pastilitos habaneros* (meat pies) or gourmet chargrilled chicken sandwiches, then finish with chocolate torte.

🚌 189 D3 ✉ 11 Ballsbridge Terrace, D4
☎ 01 660 5539; www.bella-cuba.com
🕐 Mon–Fri noon–3, Mon–Sun 5–11

Café en Seine €€

Beyond the ordinary turquoise-painted front of this restaurant and bar lies a wonderful belle époque world of marble tables and floors and skylights, adorned with statuesque lady lamps and gilt-edged mirrors. Come here for gourmet open sandwiches, salads or seafood specials at lunchtime, and then return for delicious classics such as French onion soup, risotto or rib-eye steak in the evening. There's a popular Sunday jazz brunch, as well as musical entertainment at other times. It is also good for cocktails.

🚌 191 E1 ✉ 40 Dawson Street, D2
☎ 01 677 4567; www.cafeenseine.ie
🕐 Wed–Sat noon–3am, Sun–Tue noon–1am

La Cave €€

Full of atmosphere, the capital's oldest French-style wine bar serves simple bistro fare at affordable prices with a huge wine list comprising more than 275 wines. Everything is squeezed into a tiny basement space, which is nostalgically decorated with bistro clichés – *fin-de-siècle* posters, wine labels, red-and-white checked tablecloths and candles. It is especially popular for post-theatre and late-night dining.

🚌 191 E2 ✉ 28 Anne Street South, D2
☎ 01 679 4409; www.lacavewinebar.com
🕐 Mon–Sat noon–2am, Sun 5–2am

Southside East

The Chili Club €€

This small, intimate restaurant hidden in a side street off Grafton Street was Dublin's first authentic Thai restaurant. The service is friendly and attentive, while the cuisine is genuine Thai.

✚ 191 E2
✉ 1 Anne's Lane, Anne Street South, D2
☎ 01 677 3721; www.chiliclub.ie ⏰ Tue–Fri 12:30–2:30, 5–11, Sat 5:30–11, Sun 5–10

Cornucopia €–€€

The aroma of simmering stews is irresistible at Dublin's best vegetarian restaurant. The slightly cluttered interior is just part of the appeal, second only to tasty portions of Moroccan chickpea tagine or spinach and hazelnut cannelloni, two typical dishes on the menu. The soup of the day is always good value and there are also numerous salads to choose from. Make a meal of it with a bottle of the organic house wine. A breakfast menu including buttermilk pancakes with blueberry compote is served until midday.

✚ 191 D2 ✉ 19 Wicklow Street, D02FK27
☎ 01 677 7583; www.cornucopia.ie
⏰ Mon, Tue 8:30–9, Wed–Sat 8:30–10, Sun noon–9

Diep Le Shaker €€

This light, bright, two-storey Asian restaurant near Fitzwilliam Square, with its voguish cocktail bar, modern red-and-yellow velvet chairs and starched white linen, evokes a mood of comfortable glamour and relaxed sophistication. The menu offers equally stylish cuisine: Chinese dishes are marked in blue on the menu, Thai dishes in red.

✚ 188 B4
✉ 55 Pembroke Lane (off Pembroke Street), D2
☎ 01 661 1829; www.diep.net
⏰ Tue–Fri noon–2:30, 5–10, Sat 6:30–11

L'Ecrivain €€€

Derry Clarke is undoubtedly one of Dublin's most acclaimed chefs. He is a devotee of New Irish Cuisine (➤ 47) with Mediterranean influences, and he always uses the freshest of local produce to create exquisite flavour combinations, as exemplified in his wild Irish sea trout with crayfish and avruga caviar avocado.

A further litany of delights on the dessert menu includes lemon and pinenut parfait with meringue and lemon curd, and milk chocolate brûlée. The restaurant is light, airy and sophisticated and the wine list is tremendous. The balcony is ideal for alfresco dining in summer.

✚ 188 B4 ✉ 109a Baggot Street Lower, D2
☎ 01 661 1919; www.lecrivain.com
⏰ Thu, Fri 12:30–2, Mon–Sat 6:30–10:30

Ely €–€€

This popular, contemporary wine bar occupies the ground floor and basement of a stylishly renovated Georgian town house. It serves excellent Irish fare employing top-class produce from the owner's organic farm. Options might include soup, sausage and mash, Irish stew made with organic lamb, local oysters and genuine Dublin coddle (bacon, bangers and spuds) – with 60 different wines served by the glass.

✚ 188 B4 ✉ 22 Ely Place, D2
☎ 01 676 8986; www.elywinebar.ie
⏰ Mon–Thu noon–11:30, Fri noon–12:30, Sat 5–12:30

🍴 Gourmet Burger Kitchen €

The wide selection of extra large burgers (falafel, veggie, and imaginative burgers such as mozzarella and habanero jam) is served with freshly cooked fries in a variety of flavours. There are also salads, dips, sauces and sides such as home-made onion rings. This chain may be a more expensive, Irish version of McDonalds but the burgers here are individually prepared and delicious. The popular Feast on Burgers special deal for €14.75 gets you a burger with fries and a bottomless soft drink.

✚ 190 C3
✉ Temple Bar Square, Temple Bar, D1
☎ 01 670 8343; www.gbk.ie
🕐 Sun–Wed noon–10, Thu–Sat till 11

L'Gueuleton & Hogan's Bar €€

On the east side of South Great George's Street, Fade Street has two venues so secret that they're not even numbered. Halfway down this dimly-lit side street is perhaps the hippest restaurant in town, L'Gueuleton. This French bistro has low lighting, bare brick walls, an open kitchen, with flames leaping from the steak grill, and a no reservations policy, ensuring packed tables (and sometimes a short queue). Check out the reasonably priced menu of French classics: snails in garlic butter, Toulouse sausages with choucroute and Lyonnaise potatoes, seasonal fish, chicken chasseur with cepes and tarragon. Dishes are authentic and attractively presented. The owners also run Hogan's bar next door, a good spot for an aperitif if you have to wait for a table at L'Gueuleton, or to enjoy a night cap.

✚ 191 D2 ✉ Fade Street, Dublin 2
☎ 01 675 3708; www.lgueuleton.com
🕐 Mon–Sat 12:30–4, 6–10; Sun 1–3, 6–9

Kilkenny €

This busy self-service restaurant on the first floor of the celebrated Irish design shop (▶ 117) is a great place to stop for refreshment while shopping in the area. The menu features many delicious options from wholesome quiches, rich stews, soups, sandwiches, home-baked breads and cakes, all produced using high-quality, additive-free ingredients. You'll find a range of Kilkenny's excellent preserves and dressings for sale in the store below.

✚ 191 F2 ✉ 6 Nassau Street, D2
☎ 01 677 7066; www.kilkennyshop.com
🕐 Mon–Fri 8:30–6 (also Thu 6–8), Sat 9–6, Sun 11–6

Marco Pierre White Steakhouse & Grill €€–€€€

Renowned chef Marco Pierre White has brought affordable glamour to Dublin with this steakhouse and grill. The menu includes crab and langoustines in season, superb smoked salmon and potted duck as starters, while mains include Irish steak, as well as fish options.

✚ 191 E2 ✉ 51 Dawson Street, D2
☎ 01 677 1155; www.marcopierrewhite.ie
🕐 Mon–Sat noon–midnight, Sun 1–midnight

La Mere Zou €€

This is a small, well-regarded restaurant serving classical French cuisine in an attractive Georgian basement on the north side of leafy St Stephen's Green. The ambience is rustic and relaxed – distinctly Provençale in its choice of sunny red, yellow and pale blue decor – with lavish bowls of fruit and freshly cut flowers dotted around and cafe-style newspapers on sticks. The service is friendly and efficient, with attention paid to detail, and the food represents good value (especially the lunch menus). The thoughtful wine list includes an excellent selection of French regional wines.

✚ 191 E1 ✉ 22 St Stephen's Green, D2
☎ 01 661 6669; www.lamerezou.ie
🕐 Mon–Sat noon–2:30, 6–10:30

Mongolian BBQ €

Watch the chefs as they prepare your choice of Chinese or Asian dishes on the grill. You can either help yourself to the buffet (one course is €6.90, the all-you-can-eat option is €13.90) or make a selection from the à la carte menu. Given the very reasonable prices, the quality of the food is really very good. Choose the way your meat, vegetables and fresh spices are prepared. The home-made cheesecake and baked apple crumble with vanilla ice cream are both delicious.

✚ 191 D3 ✉ 7 Anglesea Street, Temple Bar, D2
☎ 01 670 4154; www.mongolianbbq.ie
🕐 Noon–11

Southside East

One Pico €€–€€€

Owner-chef Eamonn O'Reilly keeps stacking up the awards for this fine-dining restaurant, combining a dedication for sourcing excellent local produce with culinary flair. The menu includes many inventive dishes such as langoustine risotto with a truffle foam and assiette of pork with hand-dived scallops. Choosing the set lunch menu won't break the bank.

➕ 191 E2 ✉ 5–6 Molesworth Place, Schoolhouse Lane, off St Stephen's Green, D2 ☎ 01 676 0300; www.onepico.com ⏰ Mon–Sun noon–10

Pasta Fresca €

This is a long-established restaurant-cum-delicatessen situated just off Grafton Street. The shop sells fresh pasta, sauces, oils and its own Caffe Fresca coffee, while the restaurant specializes in Italian cuisine, including a good choice of vegetarian options, delicious salads and good pizza. It's open all day, and constantly busy; the lunch deals are very popular.

➕ 191 D2 ✉ 3–4 Chatham Street, D2 ☎ 01 679 2402; www.pastafresca.ie ⏰ Mon–Thu 11:30–11:30, Fri, Sat 11:30–midnight, Sun 12:30–10

Patrick Guilbaud €€€

This is one of the top restaurants in Dublin (it's located in the Merrion Hotel; ▶ 45), with high prices to match. Renowned chef Patrick Guilbaud is celebrated for his dazzling fusion of contemporary French haute cuisine and traditional Irish influences, using superb local produce. Dining here is ultra-formal, the service is meticulous, while the food is refreshingly simple. It makes an excellent choice for a special occasion. At lunchtime it tends to be frequented by business clients.

➕ 192 B1 ✉ Merrion Hotel, 21 Merrion Street Upper, D2 ☎ 01 676 4192; www.restaurantpatrickguilbaud.ie ⏰ Tue–Sat 12:30–2:15 (Sat from 1), 7–10:15

Il Posto Restaurant €€–€€€

Tucked away down some steps, this popular Italian restaurant serves classic dishes with a modern twist using locally sourced ingredients. For lunch or an early dinner, enjoy antipasti of cured meats and caponata, followed by risotto and finishing with tiramisu, or take your time over a more elaborate four-course dinner, ending with mouth-watering desserts such as chocolate pot with poached pear.

➕ 191 E1 ✉ 10 St Stephen's Green ☎ 01 679 4769; www.ilpostorestaurant.com ⏰ Mon–Sat noon–2.30, 5:30–10

Roly's Bistro €€

Large, loud and lively, this two-storey bistro in Ballsbridge, serving French, Irish and international classics, is one of Dublin's top eateries. Dishes include Clonakilty black pudding wrapped in brioche, Kerry lamb pie, and Dublin Bay prawns with garlic, chilli and lemon. Booking is essential.

➕ 189 D3 ✉ 7 Ballsbridge Terrace, D4 ☎ 01 668 2611; www.rolysbistro.ie ⏰ Daily noon–3, 5:45–10

Shanahan's €€€

This American-style steakhouse, set in a gracious Georgian mansion, is known for its Irish Angus beef, seafood and an impressive wine list. Before your meal, enjoy an aperitif in the Oval Office – a bar decorated with memorabilia commemorating some of the American presidents with Irish connections.

➕ 191 D1 ✉ 119 St Stephen's Green, D2 ☎ 01 407 0939; www.shanahans.ie ⏰ Mon–Sat 5:30–11, Fri 12:30–2, 5:30–11

The Shelbourne Hotel €–€€

No visit to Dublin would be complete without afternoon tea at this historic hotel (▶ 46) – fancy sandwiches and cakes in the Lord Mayor's Lounge, where the Irish Constitution was written in 1922. For pre-dinner drinks, try the Horseshoe Bar, frequented by politicians, media and showbiz folk, before dining in the hotel's main restaurant, No 27 The Green.

🏛 191 F1 ✉ 27 St Stephen's Green, D2
☎ 01 663 4500
🕐 Tea 12:30–5:30, Fri, Sat noon–6:30

Thornton's €€€

The restaurant of Kevin Thornton, acknowledged as Ireland's finest chef, boasts two Michelin stars. The dining-room is pleasingly understated and the food refreshingly simple – an exquisite blend of traditional Irish and southern French cuisine – with heavenly desserts.

🏛 191 D1 ✉ Fitzwilliam Hotel (➤ 45), St Stephen's Green, D2
☎ 01 478 7008; www.thorntonsrestaurant.com
🕐 Fri, Sat 12:30–2:30, Tue–Sat 6–10

Where to...
Shop

FASHION

You'll be spoiled for choice on and around Grafton Street, Dublin's principal shopping thoroughfare. There's everything here from major British high-street chains (Next, Jigsaw, Warehouse, Monsoon, Marks & Spencer...) to international designer stores and fashionable one-off boutiques.

Try **Pamela Scott** (84 Grafton Street, D2; tel: 01 492 5888; www. pamelascott.com) for party kit and cool daywear; **Richard Alan**'s smart boutique (84 Grafton Street, D2; tel: 01 616 8907), specializing in well-known designer labels such as Betty Barclay, Escada, Valentino and other chic names; **Asha** (St Stephen's Green Shopping Centre, D2; tel: 01 478 1396) stocks alternative style clothing and rock band merchandise and accessories; and **Alias Tom** (Duke Lane, D2; tel: 01 671 5443; www.aliastom.com), a

destination for stylish men hooked on such labels as Dolce & Gabbana, Paul Smith, Issey Miyake and Prada.

Fitzpatricks Shoes (76 Grafton Street, D2; www.fitzpatricksshoes. com) offers ultra-stylish footwear for both sexes; **Carl Scarpa's** exclusive boutique (25 Grafton Street, DO2TY77; tel: 01 677 7846; www. carlscarpa.com) is filled with trendy Italian boots and shoes.

The jewel in Grafton Street's crown is **Brown Thomas** (88 Grafton Street, D2; www.brownthomas. com), Dublin's most glamorous department store, fantastic for chic fashion separates, international labels, local fashion talent, hats, shoes, linen, lingerie and cosmetics.

BT2 (28–29 Grafton Street, D2; tel: 01 605 6747), its sidekick across the street, appeals to a younger label-conscious age group, with a top reputation for unisex designer sportswear, jeans and casual wear by Tommy Hilfiger, Calvin Klein, Prada Sport, DKNY and others.

At the far end of Grafton Street, St Stephen's Green mall contains a large **Dunnes Store** (tel: 01 478 0188), a department store chain that sells clothes, household wares and groceries, while **Alphabet Kids** (138 Tritonville Road, Irishtown; tel: 01 660 3848) offers a wide selection of children's clothing and toys.

IRISH SOUVENIRS

A stone's throw from Grafton Street, in nearby Nassau Street, bordering Trinity College, a concentration of touristy gift shops conceals one or two real gems offering the finest of Irish handicrafts and knitwear, including the huge **Kilkenny Shop** (5–6 Nassau Street, D2; www. kilkennyshop.com). At the forefront of contemporary Irish design, it is among the best shops in town for stylish gifts and souvenirs. Here you'll find a dazzling choice of local fashions, pottery, jewellery, linen, arts and handicrafts to suit all tastes and budgets, from chunky Aran sweaters and traditional oak walking-sticks to the latest John Rocha Waterford crystal designs. Work by Ireland's pre-eminent potter, **Louis Mulcahy**, is also on sale here. His unfussy designs are much in demand, his luminous glazes adorning everything from stylish tableware to vast signature floor vases.

House of Ireland (37 Nassau Street, D2; tel: 01 671 1111; www.houseofireland.com) has woollens, Celtic jewellery and Waterford crystal. Nearby, the name of **Kevin & Howlin** (31 Nassau Street, D2; tel: 01 633 4576; www.kevinandhowlin.com), a long-established family firm, is synonymous with hand-woven Donegal tweed. It has a wide range of beautifully tailored jackets, waistcoats and the type of suits worn by George Bernard Shaw. Also look out for its range of classic caps, including The Great Gatsby, The Sherlock Holmes, The Quiet Man and The Dubliner, which make a great souvenir.

Insider Tip

Off Nassau Street, the **Avoca Handweavers** company (11–13 Suffolk Street, D2; www.avoca.ie, and also at Powerscourt House, Enniskerry, ► 150) produces genuine Irish products with an arty slant. Their city-centre store is a treasure-trove of stylish Irish fashion, good quality crafts, toys and gifts, topped by a cafe (► 113), which makes an ideal stop for coffee or lunch.

For up-to-the-minute streamline furniture and accessories, try **Minima** (The Waterfront, Hanover Quay, D2; tel: 01 633 7716; www.minimafurniture.co.uk); and you can't beat the shop at the archaeology branch of the **National Museum of Ireland** (tel: 01 677 7444; ► 98), which sells items of traditional Irish jewellery, such as silver sun disc brooches. In Celtic mythology the sun design was a symbol of vitality and fertility while the Celtic knot symbolizes the endlessness cycle of birth, life and death.

In a similar vein, the jeweller **Celtic Spirit** (www.celticspirit.ie), in St Stephen's Green Shopping Centre, specializes in Claddagh rings (a heart topped by a crown), Celtic crosses, harps, shamrocks and Celtic knotwork.

BOOKS

There is a wide choice of bookstores near the university, including **Hodges Figgis** (56–58 Dawson Street, D2; tel: 01 677 4754), which specializes in Irish literature and academic publications. It also has a good range of guides, fiction, children's books and an in-store coffee shop.

For rare, out of print or special editions of works by leading Irish writers, such as Yeats and Joyce, try the antiquarian bookshop **Ulysses Rare** (10 Duke Street, D2; tel: 01 671 8676; www.rarebooks.ie). You can also browse and purchase their books online. **Easons** (Ground Floor, St Stephen's Shopping Centre, D2; tel: 01 478 3060; www.easons.com) stocks an extensive range of newspapers and magazines, books about Ireland as well as the latest novels and nonfiction. Founded in Ireland in 1819, the company is still privately owned and, with dozens of stores, is the most successful bookstore chain in the country.

FOOD

Tiny **Sheridan's Cheesemongers** (11 Anne Street South, D2; www.sheridanscheesemongers.com) stocks smoked salmon and charcuterie, and locally produced artisan cheeses. If you are tempted to take a selection of these home as a souvenir, the following varieties of cheese travel well: Doolin, Carrigaline, Cooleeney Camembert, Knockalara and Brodie's Boilie (preserved in oil).

Insider Tip

Dunne & Crescenzi (14 Frederick Street South, D2; tel: 01 675 9892; www.dunneandcrescenzi.com) are the experts on Italian artisan food; and **Butler's Irish Chocolates** (51a Grafton Street, D2; tel: 01 616 7004; www.butlerschocolates.com) has a delicious pick-and-choose selection of foil-wrapped truffles, with such exotic flavours as tiramisu, apple pie, Baileys and even Guinness.

Lastly, in the renovated Grand Canal Dock, **Fresh – The Good Food Market** (Grand Canal Square, D2; tel: 01 671 8004; www.freshthe goodfoodmarket.ie) is a popular food chain inspired by farmers' markets and bursting with fresh fruit, vegetables, rustic bread, juices and coffee.

Where to...
Go Out

BARS & PUBS

Dublin's Southside has more than its fair share of chic, stylish bars. Here you can pose with the likes of Eddie Irvine and Jacques Villeneuve in **Sam's Bar** (Dawson Hotel & Spa, 35 Dawson Street, D2; tel: 01 612 7999; www.thedawson.ie)), Bono in **Searsons** (42–44 Baggot Street Lower, D2; www.searsonsbar.ie), or join the beautiful people who crowd the street-side terrace of the **Bailey** (2 Duke Street, D2; tel: 01 670 4939; www.baileybarcafe.com) and the belle époque **Café En Seine** (▶ 113), with its glass ceilings, palms and mirrors.

Older professional types head for the Shelbourne's **Horseshoe Bar** (▶ 116) near An Dáil Éireann (Irish Parliament).

Kehoe's (9 Anne Street South, D2; tel: 01 677 8312) is one of Dublin's most popular and authentic old-style pubs. Enter late at night, and you'll find raised glasses and lively conversation all around.

In a similar vein, **Mulligan's** (8 Poolbeg Street, D2; www.mulligans. ie) is reputed to serve the best pints in town. The focus is very much on the drinking.

Another landmark pub is **Davy Byrne's** (21 Duke Street, D2; www. davybyrnes.com). Even though its modern interior is disappointing, it has attracted many famous customers: revolutionary Michael Collins, Sinn Féin leader Arthur Griffith, writers Brendan Behan and Liam O'Flaherty and artist William Orpen all drank here, while Leopold Bloom, James Joyce's protagonist in the novel *Ulysses*, dropped into the "moral pub" at lunchtime for a gorgonzola cheese sandwich and a glass of burgundy.

Doheny & Nesbitt (5 Baggot Street Lower; tel: 01 676 2945; www.dohenyandnesbitts.ie) is a cosy, old-fashioned Victorian pub just around the corner from An Dáil Éireann (the Irish Parliament). It has always attracted a vivid cross-section of Dublin's movers and shakers, most notably lawyers, politicians, financiers and journalists. The bar is magnificent – antique mahogany – and there are wooden partitions for privacy.

Opposite Doheny & Nesbitt, **Toner's** (No 139 Baggot Street Lower; www.tonerspub.ie) is an authentic Victorian pub with original fixtures and fittings, including gilt mirrors, lamps and a snug, and with old-fashioned drawers that were once used for storing tea and porter.

LIVE MUSIC

The more traditional-minded can search for the perfect pint of Guinness and a bit of *craic agus ceol* (fun and music) at **O'Donoghue's** (15 Merrion Row, D2; www.odonoghues. ie), where the famous ballad group The Dubliners began their musical career in the early 1960s, along with Christy Moore, and where impromptu sessions are still a regular feature of the pub.

On Wednesday and Sunday nights **McDaid's** (Harry Street, D2; tel: 01 679 4395) sometimes has live music by the resident blues band. Once the "local" of Brendan Behan, Flann O'Brien and Patrick Kavanagh, this great literary pub beside the Westbury Hotel draws an eclectic crowd of tourists, bookish types and young Dubliners to its cosy interior.

Marking the return of cocktail culture to Dublin **The Sugar Club** (8 Leeson Street Lower, D2; www.thesugarclub.com) offers live swing, jazz, salsa and blues, but its programme is varied and also includes pop and folk, burlesque and stand-up. For mellow late-night sounds seek out **JJ Smyth's** (12 Aungier Street, D2; www.jjsmyths.com) which offers live performances by talented jazz and blues musicians.

NIGHTCLUBS

The Southside East area abounds in lively nightspots, one of which is **Dtwo** (60 Harcourt Street, D2; tel: 01 476 4604; www.dtwonightclub.com) a bar, beer garden and nightclub. The popular all-weather beer garden, Backyard BBQ, takes up two floors and can accommodate up to 500 guests. The nightclub in the basement has up to 3 DJs playing a cross section of music from the 1970s and 80s as well as electro, house and funk.

The stylishly **Krystle Nightclub** (Russell Court Hotel, 21–25 Harcourt Street, D2; tel: 01 478 4066) mostly appeals to a younger business crowd and its two bars serves all the usual drinks and cocktails. The hotel's heated Beer Garden terrace is open all year and is one of Dublin's hippest spots.

A venue operating a strict door policy is **Lillie's Bordello** (Adam Court, Grafton Street, D2; www.lilliesbordello.ie), a long-established and popular nightclub catering for more mainstream dance sounds and attracting an older clientele. Lillie's is popular with visiting musicians, film stars and celebrities.

Club Nassau (1–2 Nassau Street, D2; www.kildarestreethoteldublin.com) hosts popular 80s nights for those who want to dance and party until late. In Leeson Street you'll find a handful of basement bars, several of which remain open until around 3am. The drinks aren't cheap, but they will serve you the latest "last orders" in Dublin.

THEATRE & CLASSICAL MUSIC

The **Gaiety** (46 King Street South, D2; www.gaietytheatre.ie) is the main theatre in this part of town, staging mainstream productions, especially works by well-known Irish playwrights, but also musicals, ballet, opera and, in season, pantomime. After hours, this jewel of Victorian architecture opens its doors as a hugely successful late-night club. The auditorium is used to screen classic black-and-white movies, while the rest of the premises (three floors and five bars) occasionally hosts themed live-music nights of salsa, jazz, soul, and R 'n' B.

Given Dublin's strong musical pedigree, it's hardly surprising there is a top-notch classical music scene in the city. It centres on the **National Concert Hall** (Earlsfort Terrace, D2; www.nch.ie), home to the National Symphony Orchestra, which plays here every Friday from November to May. It also offers a varied programme of opera, chamber music, jazz and all kinds of dance.

In the heart of the Dockland area on the south side of the Liffey is the modern **Bord Gáis Energy Theatre** (Grand Canal Square, D2; http://bordgaisenergytheatre.ie) offering Broadway and West End musicals, international opera stars, classic plays (*The Mousetrap*) and prestigious Irish music and dance shows (*Riverdance*).

Northside

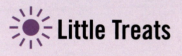 **Little Treats**

Historic Kitchen Garden

The beautifully restored Victorian Walled Garden is only a very small part of the massive **Phoenix Park** (► 126)

Thrilling Bird's-eye View

Those with a head for heights will enjoy the **Croke Park** (► 138) Skyline tour with panoramic viewing points.

Irish Coffee

The **Insomnia coffee shop** chain is 100% Irish owned and serves some of the best coffee in town; try the one in the chq Building (► 138).

Northside

Getting Your Bearings

Northside (north of the Liffey) was the last part of the city to be developed, during the 18th century. Although considered less fashionable than Southside, it none the less boasts O'Connell Street, the widest and longest thoroughfare; the tallest building; some of the finest, most fashionable Georgian houses; and such majestic edifices as Gandon's splendid Four Courts and Custom House, both situated along the north Liffey quays and regarded by many as the city's most beautiful buildings.

The view across the River Liffey to the Custom House

The main Northside sights embrace all that is typical of Dublin's culture – story-telling, literature, drama, dance, song, even drinking at the Old Jameson Distillery.

Dublin boasts a star-studded cast of writers, and the Dublin Writers Museum and the James Joyce Cultural Centre, both on the Northside, are dedicated primarily to writers who spent most of their lives here. Ireland's two most celebrated theatres – the Abbey and the Gate – keep the Irish theatre tradition alive, while a thriving music scene, both traditional and modern, flourishes in pubs and the 3Arena.

GLASNEVIN

Glasnevin Cemetery **43**

National Botanic Gardens **44**

Griffith Avenue

Drumcondra Street

The Casino, Marino

MARINO

CABRA

Cabra Road

PHIBSBOROUGH

Clonliffe Road

Croke Park Experience **42**

Aughrim St

Dorset Street

Parnell Street

Phoenix Park **8**

National Museum of Ireland – Decorative Arts & History **32**

Sheriff Street

Docklands **41**

River Liffey

0   500 m
0   500 yd

TOP 10

⭐ Phoenix Park ➤ 126

Don't Miss

At Your Leisure

Throughout the area, there is a characteristic mixture of the old with the new: Smithfield market and the dockland area have been rejuvenated; pedestrianization is creating new spaces for street events; new shops, theatres, museums and entertainment centres have sprung up. Northside may be a late developer, but there's no denying it is rapidly catching up with the Southside.

The Perfect Day

If you're not quite sure where to begin your travels, this itinerary recommends a practical and enjoyable day in Northside, taking in some of the best places to see. For more information see the main entries (► 126–139).

🕘 9:00am

Start the day with a pleasant stroll in **Phoenix Park** (below; ► 126), one of the largest city parks in the world and home to the president of Ireland. You may spot a couple of deer grazing among the trees or come upon a polo match or a game of hurling in full swing. A visit to **Dublin Zoo** (► 127) here is an absolute must for children.

Glasnevin Cemetery · **43** · **44** National Botanic Gardens · The Casino Marin· · **42** Croke P Experie· · Phoenix Park · **8** · **32** · Dockla· · **National Museum of Ireland – Decorative Arts & History**

🕚 11:00am

A short walk along the Liffey brings you to Collins Barracks, which now houses the **32 National Museum of Ireland – Decorative Arts & History** (► 129).

🕧 12:30pm

If whiskey is your tipple, take a fascinating tour through the **35 Old Jameson Distillery** (► 132), just off **34 Smithfield** (► 132), Europe's largest cobbled square, and round it off with a glass of the strong stuff.

🕜 1:30pm

Head down the quays to the heart of the little Italian Quarter and **Enoteca Delle Langhe** (► 140) for some tasty antipasti and a nice glass of Italian red.

🕒 3:00pm

Catch bus No 90 from Arran Quay to the southern end of **33 O'Connell Street** (► 130), then walk up Dublin's main and undeniably impressive thoroughfare, dominated by the **General Post Office** (► 131), book-ended by statues of two great Irish leaders, Daniel O'Connell (► 21) and Charles Stewart Parnell (► 58 and 127).

Pass the millennium **Spire of Dublin** (*Monument of Light*), and the statue of James Joyce (on the corner with Earl Street), then continue on to Parnell Square with its graceful Georgian mansions.

🕒 3:30pm
Explore Dublin's extraordinary literary past at the **38** **Dublin Writers Museum** (► 134), where all the city's best-known writers – Joyce, Shaw, Stoker, Yeats, Beckett and Behan to name a few – are documented.

🕒 5:00pm
Have a drink in a pub. Book in advance for a pre-show meal at **The Winding Stair** (► 141), an excellent eatery overlooking Ha'Penny Bridge. Then, take in a show at Ireland's national theatre, the **Abbey** (► 144) or, equally famous, the **Gate** (► 144). Otherwise head east to the **41** **Docklands** (► 138) and a night out at one of the new venues in The Point Village.

Northside

⭐8 Phoenix Park

Phoenix Park is one of the most magnificent city parks in Europe. Laid out in the mid-17th century, it is the green lung of Dublin – a vast expanse of woodland, lakes, hillocks, streams, monuments, formal gardens and ponds in the city centre – and a popular haunt of Dubliners seeking respite from the urban life.

At 707ha (1,750 acres), Phoenix Park is Europe's largest enclosed city park, five times the size of London's Hyde Park and double the size of Central Park in New York. It was created in 1663, following instructions from King Charles II "to enclose with a stone wall the lands of our ancient inheritance…and to store with deer". It was presented to the City of Dublin in 1745 for use as a public park. Today, the boundary wall is a staggering 11km (7mi) long, with eight gates for vehicles and six pedestrian entrances, and the park still contains around 500 deer.

The Wellington Memorial in the park

There is a lively and entertaining exhibition on the history of the park and its wildlife at the 👥 **visitor centre**, including an audio-visual presentation on Phoenix Park through the Ages and a special children's section where youngsters can explore the wonders of life in the forest.

Adjoining the centre is **Ashtown Castle**, a medieval towerhouse. The castle was only uncovered in the 1980s when it was found during the demolition of Ashton Lodge, a more recent building constructed around the original tower. When the deer park was laid out for King Charles II, the castle passed to a keeper whose job it was to "prevent the spoil and embezzlement of the vert or the venison". Nowadays you can visit both the castle and its miniature maze.

Sports
Phoenix Park has long been a popular sporting ground,

Relaxing in the park

and it's a common sight to see joggers, children practising hurling skills, horse-riders from local stables, or perhaps a friendly game of Gaelic football being played on the rough open ground. Also within the park is a motor-racing circuit where, in the 1920s, Grand Prix races were held; Nine Acres, the home to the Irish Polo Club (with games most Wednesday, Saturday and Sunday afternoons from May to September); and Phoenix Cricket Club, founded in 1830 and the oldest cricket club in the country.

Áras an Uachtaráin

Among the park's impressive mansions, the residence of Áras an Uachtáráin started life as a glorified park-keeper's residence. It was later remodelled by Frances Johnston, the architect of the neoclassical General Post Office (▶ 131), and for years housed various British viceroys. Following the establishment of the Irish Free State, it became home to the Governor General and eventually, in 1938, the official residence of the first Irish President, Dr Douglas Hyde. The house is open to the public on Saturdays.

THE NOTORIOUS PHOENIX PARK MURDERS

On 6 May, 1882, Lord Cavendish, the Chief Secretary in Ireland, and Thomas Burke, the Under Secretary, were stabbed to death in the park, and the name of Charles Stewart Parnell, leader of the Irish Home Rule Party, was put forward as prime suspect in an attempt to ruin his political career. Back in England, the assassination caused a furore in Westminster, and the question of Home Rule for Ireland was seriously debated. It was later revealed that the brutal knifings were committed by a secret society called the Invincibles, a radical Nationalist movement.

Dublin Zoo

One of Phoenix Park's biggest draws is Dublin Zoo. When it was founded in 1830, its only occupant was a solitary wild boar – hard to believe as you stroll around today's 24ha (60 acres) of landscaped grounds with its 700-plus animals and tropical birds from all corners of the world, many of which are rare or endangered species. Most of the animals were either born in captivity or orphaned in the wild where they faced an uncertain future, and many – including the snow leopards, gorillas and golden lion tamarinds – are part of a global plan to preserve and protect these rare animals. Be sure to visit the World of Cats, World of Primates, Fringes of the Arctic and the African Plains, and you can keep the kids amused on the zoo train or at the petting farm. You can also watch the animals being fed during the daily Meet the Keeper programme, and visit the Discovery Centre to learn more about the animals, and the zoo's successful breeding and conservation programmes. The original MGM lion was filmed at Dublin Zoo.

Insider Tip

WHAT'S IN A NAME

Curiously, the park is not named after the mythical bird, but rather it is said to derive from the Gaelic *fionn uisce*, meaning "clear water", referring to a spring in the Furry Glen, near the Phoenix Column which, to add confusion, is topped by a statue of a phoenix!

TAKING A BREAK

The **Fionn Uisce** restaurant in the grounds of the visitor centre is good for lunch, and the **Phoenix Park tea rooms** outside the zoo for snacks, coffees and teas but, on sunny days, it's hard to beat a picnic.

✚ 182 A2 ✉ Phoenix Park, D8; www.phoenixpark.ie
🚌 10, 25, 26, 37, 38, 39, 46A, 70 🕐 Open 24 hours

Dublin Zoo
☎ 01 474 8900; www.dublinzoo.ie
🕐 Mar–Sep daily 9:30–6; Oct daily 9:30–5:30; Nov–Jan daily 9:30–4;
Feb daily 9:30–5. Last admission one hour before closing
💶 €17, children €12.20

Visitor Centre
☎ 01 677 0095
🕐 Apr–Dec daily 10–6; Jan–Mar daily 9:30–5:30, last admission 4:45.
Áras an Uachtaráin: free guided tours every Sat 10:30–3:30 on the hour (tickets from visitor centre)
💶 Free. Entry to Ashdown Castle and Áras an Uachtaráin by guided tour only
🚲 Bicycle rental available at southwest park entrance

INSIDER INFO

Insider Tip

Allow an hour to visit the visitor centre and Ashtown Castle, and a good couple of hours to visit the zoo. There is plenty to do and see in the park:

■ The park's deer are best spotted around **Fifteen Acres**, a wide expanse of grassland, and **Oldtown Wood**, one of the largest woodland areas.

■ The only cultivated part of the park is the **People's Garden**, a Victorian-style garden with an attractive pond.

■ The **Wellington Testimonial** is a 63m (207ft) obelisk of Wicklow granite with bronze bas-reliefs made from captured French cannon depicting scenes from the Duke's battles.

■ The **Papal Cross** was erected to commemorate the mass conducted here by Pope John Paul II to more than a million people in September 1979.

32 National Museum of Ireland – Decorative Arts & History

Housed in two wings of the Collins Barracks, the Decorative Arts & History branch of the National Museum of Ireland provides a fascinating insight into Ireland's economic, social, political and military progress through the centuries.

The collection comprises around 2,500 objects ranging from weaponry, furniture, folk-life items and costume to silver, ceramics and glassware. It forms part of the National Museum of Ireland collection together with the Archaeology Museum (▶ 98) and the Natural History Museum (▶ 111).

Don't miss the **Curator's Choice Exhibition**, where 25 objects chosen by the curators of the various collections are on display. These include a 2,000-year-old Japanese ceremonial bell, the gauntlets worn by King William at the Battle of the Boyne (▶ 154), and a 15th-century hurling ball made of hair. Other highlights include the Fonthill vase, one of the earliest pieces of Chinese porcelain; 19th-century neo-Celtic furniture; and a fashion exhibition.

A major exhibition is **Soldiers and Chiefs** with military and personal items building up a picture of soldiering and warfare from 1550 onwards. Also interesting, an exhibition on the events of the 1916 **The Easter Rising**. It includes an original copy of the Proclamation of the Republic and an illuminated manuscript, *Book of the Resurrection*, commemorating those who died in the struggle for Irish independence.

The austere but impressive Collins Barracks now houses part of the National Museum

TAKING A BREAK
Soup Dragon (▶ 141) for a selection of home-made soups.

✚ 183 E1 ✉ Collins Barracks, Benburb Street, D7
☎ 01 677 7444; www.museum.ie 🕒 Tue–Sat 10–5, Sun 2–5
🚌 25, 25A, 66, 67, 79; free shuttle to the National Museum of Ireland 🎫 Free

33 O'Connell Street

The ghosts of Dublin's past are everywhere in the city, but perhaps nowhere more so than O'Connell Street, with its monuments and historic public buildings. This impressive, tree-lined boulevard marks the very centre of the city.

Important Figures

Monuments mark each end of the street. Close to the O'Connell Bridge is one to **Daniel O'Connell** (➤ 21), who secured Catholic emancipation in 1829. The allegorical statues of *Four Winged Victories* around the base symbolize O'Connell's qualities of Courage, Fidelity, Eloquence and Patriotism, while the figures around the pedestal represent the Church, the professions, the arts and the labouring classes, and Erin, holding up the Act of Emancipation. When the monument was erected in 1882, the street was called Sackville Street. The name changed to O'Connell Street in 1924.

The General Post Office – scene of the notorious Easter Rising

- The **statue of James Larkin**
  (►22) depicts the great
  trade unionist in full flow,
  championing the workers'
  rights. His fundamental
  message appears on the
  plinth: "The great appear
  great because we are on
  our knees. Let us arise."

- The 120m (400-ft) *Spire
  of Dublin – Monument of
  Light* is seven times the
  height of the GPO oppo-
  site. Its tip is illuminated
  from a light source within
  to provide a beacon in the
  night sky.

**Inside the
General Post
Office today**

The northern end of O'Connell Street is
marked by a monument to **Charles Stewart
Parnell** (►127), the 19th-century leader
of the struggle for Irish Home Rule. **Parnell
Square** beyond, which was laid out in 1755,
was the city's second Georgian square after
St Stephen's Green (►104). Among the
elegant buildings lining the square are Dublin City Gallery
The Hugh Lane (►134), the Dublin Writers Museum
(►134), the Rotonda Maternity Hospital and the Gate
Theatre (►140). In the centre of the square, the Garden
of Remembrance (►35) is dedicated to those who gave
their lives for Irish independence; a statue depicts the Irish
myth of the *Children of Lir* by Oisín Kelly. Developments
in the 1960s and 70s left little of Dublin's Georgian architecture standing on O'Connell Street.

The Easter Rising

The grand Palladian-style **General Post Office** (GPO) was
the headquarters of the Irish Volunteers during the Easter
Rising of 1916. From its steps, Pádraic Pearse (►22)
proclaimed Ireland's independence, but a week later the
Rising had been crushed. Inside are a pictorial account of
the Rising, and an iconic sculpture of the mythical hero
Cú Chulainn commemorating the men.

➕ 191 E5   ✉ O'Connell Street, D1
🚌 Cross-city buses   🚊 LUAS: Abbey Street

INSIDER INFO

- O'Connell Street is not only historically significant but it also offers some of the
  best shopping north of the Liffey (►141).
- **O'Connell Bridge** has the unusual distinction of being broader than it is long. It also
  affords impressive city vistas.
- **Number 42** is the last remaining Georgian house on the street, now part of the Royal
  Dublin Hotel.

**Insider
Tip**

At Your Leisure

long-established **horse market** – not thoroughbreds, but rather a more rural spectacle of scruffy ponies and mules with young children riding them bareback over the cobblestones while adults negotiate the price.

Smithfield has undergone a major face-lift. It now has a smart new retail and cultural centre dominated by the Old Jameson Distillery, with additional attractions relocating to the square. Throughout the year Smithfield is a venue for events and activities including concerts, markets, a Chinese Carnival during Chinese New Year and an **open-air ice rink** at Christmas.

🚏 187 E5 ✉ Smithfield Square, D7
🚌 25, 25A, 67, 67A (from Abbey Street Middle) 68, 69, 79 (from Aston Quay), 90 (from Connolly, Tara and Heuston Stations)
🚋 LUAS: Smithfield

Smithfield Square is the heart of a regenerated area

34 Smithfield

Smithfield Square is the largest cobbled square in Europe. Originally laid out in the mid-17th century as a cattle marketplace, for centuries the area was a bustling place of business where traders and merchants sold their wares. Corn and seed brokers abounded, and cattle and potato stores dotted the streetscape. Smithfield retained its place as Dublin's main market until the late 1880s.

On the first Sunday of March and September it still hosts a

35 Old Jameson Distillery

Think Dublin, think *Guinness*. Yet the city has an equally venerable tradition of whiskey production. Jameson whiskey has been distilled here since 1780. Today, Jameson is not only the highest-selling Irish whiskey in the world, but also the fastest-growing spirit brand.

The Old Jameson Distillery may no longer be in use, but you can relive the past at the visitor centre. The visit includes a short film called *Uisce Beatha* (The Water of Life) on the history of Irish whiskey, from the sixth century to the present day. This is followed by a guided tour around a detailed reconstruction of the old working distillery to see the unique art of Irish whiskey-making.

The tour culminates in the Jameson bar, where you will be given a chance to compare Irish whiskey with Scotch and Bourbon. Irish whiskey is unique in the whisky world (note spelling; only Irish whiskey has the "e") because it is distilled three times. This provides the smooth, distinctive taste that distinguishes it from Scotch and Bourbon (many whiskys are distilled only once, Scotch is distilled twice).

🕂 187 E5 ✉ Bow Street, Smithfield, D7
☎ 01 807 2355; www.jamesonwhiskey.com
🕐 Daily 9–6:30 (last tour 5:30)
🚌 25, 25A, 25B, 66, 66A, 67, 67A, 68, 69, 79, 90
🚊 LUAS: Smithfield 💶 €15

36 Four Courts

One of Dublin's most striking buildings, the Four Courts has been at the heart of Ireland's legal system for over 200 years. As the name suggests, there were originally four courts here but these were reduced to two during the 19th-century restructuring, and only the Supreme Court and High Court remain.

It was designed in the late 18th century by James Gandon, architect of Custom House and the Bank of Ireland building in College Green, and the similarity of styles is very apparent. Facing the Liffey, its portico features six Corinthian columns supporting a pediment topped by three Classical statues of Moses, Justice and Mercy. There are two further statues of Wisdom and Authority at either end of the building, which is topped by a colonnaded dome.

The building was severely damaged during the Civil War. While the exterior was rebuilt and

The colonnaded dome of the Four Courts, overlooking the River Liffey

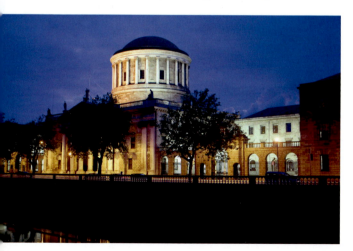

Northside

remodelled, the interiors were never restored to their former glory.

✚ 190 A3 ✉ Four Courts, Inns Quay
🕐 Not open to the public

37 Dublin City Gallery – The Hugh Lane

The Municipal Gallery of Modern Art is situated in Charlemont House, one of Dublin's finest Georgian buildings. Formerly a town house owned by Lord Charlemont, a connoisseur and patron of the arts, it was first opened to the public in 1930 to display the treasured Impressionist paintings of collector Sir Hugh Lane.

The entrance hall contains some noteworthy 20th-century Irish installation work, including Patrick O'Reilly's *Wringer*, and *Monkey and Dog* by John Kindness, depicting the sectarian conflict in Northern Ireland by use of simile, with "a menacing Republican dog locked in combat with a conceited Orange monkey". Beyond, the sculpture gallery exhibits works by Rodin, Epstein, Degas and Moore. The next gallery contains a fine collection of paintings by Dublin-born "impressionists", Jack B Yeats, William Leech, Walter Osborne and others. Hugh Lane's French Impressionist paintings hang in a

small room to the left of the sculpture gallery, and include Claude Monet's *Waterloo Bridge* and Renoir's celebrated *Les Parapluies*.

The gallery was also endowed with the entire studio of Francis Bacon at 7 Reece Mews, London by Bacon's sole heir, John Edwards.
The Francis Bacon Studio – his work and living space for the last 30 years of his life – has been reconstructed, together with an audio-visual room recording the removal and reconstruction process. The museum stages temporary exhibitions on the first floor. There is also a cafe and gift shop.

The Hugh Lane expanded to allow a more substantial exhibition of the permanent collection as well as providing specially designed galleries for the temporary exhibition programme. There is also an education resource room and lectures facility on the site.

✚ 183 F2
✉ Charlemont House, Parnell Square North, D1
☎ 01 222 5550; www.hughlane.ie
🕐 Tue–Thu 10–6, Fri–Sat 10–5, Sun 11–5
🚌 7, 11, 11B, 13, 16, 38, 40, 46A 🎫 Free

38 Dublin Writers Museum

This museum is a must for anyone who is interested in Dublin's immense literary heritage. Ireland has produced a surprising number of the world's greatest writers and here, inside a beautiful 18th-century town house, all the best-known

The fine Georgian facade of the Dublin City Gallery

The Writers Museum (above) and one of the books on display (below)

writers of the city – Jonathan Swift, George Bernard Shaw, Bram Stoker, James Joyce, WB Yeats, Samuel Beckett, Flan O'Brien, Brendan Behan and many others – are featured, together with letters, manuscripts, photographs, rare books, paintings, personal belongings and other memorabilia. Of particular note are Oliver St John Gogarty's flying goggles; James

OFF THE BEATEN TRACK
A visit to **St Michan's Church** (tel: 01 872 4154; Mar–Oct Mon–Fri 10–12:30, 2–4:30, Sat 10–12:45; entry fee €4) is only for the brave, for in the crypt of this church lie the mummified remains of John and Henry Sheares, Barristers of Law, executed for their part in the Irish Rebellion of 1798. The guide provides the full gory account of what happened to them.

Joyce's animal-embroidered waistcoat; portrait photographs of Oscar Wilde and Samuel Beckett by the sea; and such celebrated first editions as *Ulysses, The Dubliners and Dracula*.

The museum holds exhibitions and readings and has a special room devoted to children's literature. There is also a library of rare books, a gallery of portraits and busts, a Zen garden, a bookshop and a cafe.

➕ 183 F2 ✉ 18–19 Parnell Square North, D1
☎ 01 872 2077; www.writersmuseum.com
🕐 Sep–May Mon–Sat 10–5, Sun 11–5;
Jun–Aug Mon–Fri 10–6
🚌 1, 11, 16, 46A, 120, 122, 145 💰 €7.50

39 James Joyce Centre

More than any other Irish writer, James Joyce (1882–1941) celebrated the character of the capital in his work, and this centre, housed in a beautifully restored Georgian town house, is dedicated to his life and work. Among manuscripts and memorabilia is a set of biographies of around 50 characters from Joyce's most famous novel, *Ulysses*, all based on real Dublin people. You can also watch short films on Joyce and listen to recordings of him reading from his works.

A display at the James Joyce Centre

JOYCE'S DUBLIN
Much of Joyce's Dublin still survives and fans of Leopold Bloom, the hero of *Ulysses*, can retrace his footsteps around the city on 16 June, 1904, with the assistance of the Ulysses Map of Dublin (available from Dublin Tourism, ▶ 41). Bloom's lunchtime route through the city centre is marked by a series of 14 bronze pavement plaques, running from the Evening Telegraph Office in Prince's Street to the National Museum (▶ 98).

The centre also organizes walking tours of Joyce's Dublin (▶ panel) and, in the courtyard of the centre, is a striking mural based on *Ulysses* and the door of No 7 Eccles Street – the fictional home of Leopold and Molly Bloom.

➕ 184 A2
✉ 35 North Great George's Street, D1
☎ 01 878 8547; www.jamesjoyce.ie
🕐 Mon–Sat 10–5, Sun noon–5 🚌 1, 4, 7, 8, 9, 11, 13, 16, 38, 40, 44, 63, 118, 120, 123
🚊 LUAS: Abbey Street 💰 €5

40 Custom House

The Custom House, designed by James Gandon (1743–1823) to replace the old customs point further up the River Liffey, is considered by many to be the most magnificent building in Dublin. This beautifully

James Gandon's Custom House

proportioned Georgian masterpiece, with its splendid portico of Doric columns and a 38m (125ft) copper dome, took 10 years to build, during which Gandon had to overcome many obstacles.

Gandon's first setback was the marshy ground alongside the Liffey. This he overcame by employing an innovative form of raft foundation, which brought him international acclaim. His second problem was ongoing opposition to the scheme. He received threatening letters from opponents (and therefore carried a sword when visiting the site) and in 1789 a mysterious fire damaged the partially completed edifice.

The building continued to be targeted after its completion. There was a further fire in 1833, and in 1921 the IRA torched the building during the War of Independence. It was restored in time for the Custom House bicentenary in 1991. From the outside, the best view of the Custom House is from George's Quay, on the opposite side of the river. Note the arms

Insider Tip

of Ireland crowning the two pavilions and a series of 14 allegorical heads depicting Ireland's main rivers and the Atlantic Ocean. Atop the copper dome is the statue of Commerce.

Custom House now houses the Department of the Environment and only the visitor centre is open to the public.

🖾 192 B4 ⊠ Custom House Quay, D1
🕐 Visitor Centre: mid-Mar to Oct Mon–Fri 10–12:30, Sat–Sun 2–5; Nov to mid-Mar Wed–Fri 10–12:30 🚇 DART: Tara Street
💶 €1.50, family ticket €3

Further Afield

41 Docklands

The decade-long resurrection of the Liffey's Docklands, once a post-industrial wasteland, is due to conclude. On the north side of the river, now crossed by two extra bridges, the development is concentrated at the Point Village, an entertainment complex which will eventually sit in the gaze of the Watchtower, a twin funnel-shaped tower with restaurants and superb views over the sea and city. But there's plenty to see before you reach here and it's all within a half-hour walk of Custom House. Your first stop will be the **Famine Memorial**, a sculpture of life-size but waif-like figures by Rowan Gillespie, commemorating the Great Famine of the 19th century. Eastwards along the Liffey is the **chq Building**, a smart shopping complex with a glass facade. Crossing the Liffey here is the Sean O'Casey footbridge but the best is yet to come: the wing-like **Samuel Beckett bridge** at Macken Street, by the celebrated Catalan architect Santiago Calatrava.

Next to the bridge is the **National Conference Centre**, identified by its "wonky barrel" appearance. Finally, the **Point Village**, a stylish shopping plaza and entertainment area awaits completion. The **3Arena** (formerly the Point Theatre) music and entertainment venue is already up and running and the **Dublin Wheel** newly installed. Other projects planned for Point Village have been temporarily shelved due to the economic climate.

🚇 185 E1 ✉ The Point Village, Docklands
☎ 01 856 0733; www.pointvillage.ie

42 👥 Croke Park Experience (GAA Museum)

This state-of-the-art interactive museum under the stands at Croke Park, the headquarters of the Gaelic Athletic Association (GAA), provides an insight into Ireland's unique national games: hurling and Gaelic football. Amid trophies, colourful kits and ancient hurleys (hurling sticks), the ground floor follows the chronological story of the games, while the links with the nation's history are powerfully told in film. Upstairs, try your luck at interactive kicking or pucking, or test your athletic reflexes and watch thrilling excerpts from some of the classic All-Ireland hurling and football finals. With so much to see and do, allow a match-long period for your visit! There are daily stadium tours except on match days for an extra charge.

🚇 184 B3 ✉ Croke Park, D3 (entrance under the Cusack Stand, via Clonliffe Road)
☎ 01 819 2323; www.crokepark.ie
🕐 Mon–Sat 9:30–5, Sun 10:30–5, late opening Jul–Aug Mon–Sat 9:30–6 (except Sun match days when the museum is open to stand ticket-holders only, noon–3)
🎫 €6, €12 (stadium tour) 🚌 7, 11, 16, 53, 123

43 Glasnevin Cemetery

Glasnevin Cemetery opened in 1832, primarily to allow Catholics a place of burial following the abolition of the Penal Laws in 1829. Today, 4km (2.5mi) from the centre, on 49 landscaped hectares (121 acres), the cemetery has become a national institution. It is Ireland's largest graveyard, and the final resting place of more than a million people. From the paupers' graves

Programmes displayed at the GAA Museum

Michael Collins' tomb at Glasnevin

from the time of the Great Famine and those of cholera victims of the 1840s to ornately carved Celtic crosses, elaborate Gothic mausoleums and the tombs of Daniel O'Connell (➤ 21), Michael Collins (➤ 72), Eámon de Valera (➤ 22), Charles Stewart Parnell (➤ 127), William Butler Yeats (➤ 19) and Brendan Behan (➤ 19), this corner of Dublin reflects the social, political and cultural history of the last two centuries.

➕ 183 E4 ✉ Finglas Road, Glasnevin, D11
☎ 01 882 6500; www.glasnevintrust.ie
🕐 Daily 10–5. Tours: daily 11:30, 2:30 and (Jun–Aug only) 1pm
🚌 13, 19, 19A (from O'Connell Street to Harts Corner plus 5 minutes' walk), 40, 40D (from Parnell Street to Finglas Road)
🎟 €10; €6 (museum only); €12 (museum & tour)

44 National Botanic Gardens

Established in 1795, the National Botanic Gardens are the country's premier centre of botany and horticulture, but to most Dubliners they are simply a popular weekend destination for a gentle stroll amid 20,000 species of flora. Highlights include the glorious herbaceous displays; Victorian carpet bedding; vegetable gardens; the renowned rose garden; the yew walk and an arboretum with hundreds of tall specimen trees.

Statue outside The Casino at Marino

At Your Leisure

Late spring and summer are the best seasons to visit, but even in winter there is plenty to see, thanks to the dazzling displays in the cast-iron glasshouses, built in 1843 by Dublin iron-master Richard Turner. Here you will find banana trees, bamboo, Amazonian creepers, orchids, cacti, a rare collection of cycads and, in the Aquatic House, giant Amazonian water lilies.

➕ 183 F4 ✉ Glasnevin, D09VY63
☎ 01 804 0300; www.botanicgardens.ie
🕐 Daily 9–5 in summer, 9–4:30 in winter. Glasshouses open restricted hours
🚌 4, 9, 83 to Botanic Road 🎟 Free

45 The Casino, Marino

This charming little villa in the suburb of Marino, just 5km (3mi) north of the city centre, is considered among Dublin's most intriguing buildings, and one of the finest examples of Palladian architecture in Ireland – full of quirky design foibles, including hollow columns to accommodate drainpipes. The Casino (meaning "small house") was designed by Sir William Chambers in the 1760s for Lord Charlemont, and contains 16 elegantly decorated rooms. Entry is by guided tour only.

➕ 185 D4
✉ Off the Malahide road, Marino, D3
☎ 01 833 1618; www.heritageireland.ie
🕐 Mar–Oct daily 10–5; last entry 4:15
🚌 14, 27, 27B (from Eden Quay), 42, 42A, 42B (from Lower Abbey Street), 123 Imp bus from O'Connell Street
🚆 DART: Clontarf Road 🎟 €4

Where to...
Eat and Drink

Prices
Expect to pay for a three-course meal, excluding drinks but including VAT
€ under €30   €€ €30–€50   €€€ over €50

---

101 Talbot €
A friendly, first-floor restaurant that is popular with theatre-goers from the nearby Abbey and Gate theatres, 101 Talbot serves a healthy mix of Mediterranean- and Middle Eastern-inspired dishes. <mark>The simple décor is enlivened by contemporary art, which is for sale.</mark>

➕ 191 E5 ✉ 101 Talbot Street, D1
☎ 01 874 5011; www.101talbot.ie
🕐 Tue–Sat noon–3, 5–11

Chapter One Restaurant and Café €€
This stylish, brightly coloured Michelin-starrred restaurant serves modern Irish cuisine in the arched basement of the Dublin Writers Museum. Original stonework, mirrors, drapes and paintings of literary celebrities add to the ambience. By day the restaurant is full of local business people. By night, the two-course pre-theatre menu is popular, and the service is obliging – dessert and coffee can be completed after the performance.
➕ 190 C5 ✉ 18–19 Parnell Square, D1
☎ 01 873 2266; www.chapteronerestaurant.com
🕐 Tue–Fri 12:30–2, 7:30–10:30, Sat 7–10:30

Chilli Banana €–€€
This Thai restaurant is the perfect option after a match at Croke Park. Fill up on vegetarian spring rolls, spicy tom yum soup and chilli duck dishes. Early bird menus available.
➕ 184 B4 ✉ 112 Drumcondra Road, D9
☎ 01 797 9239; www.chillibanana.ie
🕐 Daily 5–10:30

The Church €€
Set over four levels, this former church now houses a club, terrace, cafe, bar and restaurant. Stop for coffee and snacks in the cafe, drinks and buffalo wings or sausages and mash in the bar, or soups, beef and ale pie, steaks and seafood in the restaurant.
➕ 190 C4
✉ Jervis Street and Mary Street, D1
☎ 01 828 0102: www.thechurch.ie
🕐 Daily 5–11

Enoteca Delle Langhe €–€€
The newly developed "Quartier Bloom" is a little Italian quarter on Ormond Quay with a few casual eateries around a communal plaza area. Delle Langhe is at the heart of the quarter, and offers an authentic *enoteca* experience of affordable Italian wines and a selection of antipasti.
➕ 190 C4 ✉ Blooms Lane, D1
☎ 01 888 0834; www.wallacewinebars.ie
🕐 Mon–Sat 12:30–midnight

Halo (Morrison Grill) €€€
This restaurant in the Morrison Hotel (▶ 46), designed by John Rocha with velvet throws, dramatic spot lighting and clean crisp lines, is one of the trendiest dining-rooms in town. An exciting menu of Asian-influenced fusion food is perfectly complemented by the relaxed yet impeccable service, making dining here a memorable experience. There are regular and popular Open Kitchen dinners with chef Richie Wilson demonstrating dishes in front of the diners.

🔲 190 C3
✉ Morrison Hotel, Ormond Quay Lower, D1
☎ 01 887 2458
🕐 Sun–Thu noon–10, Fri, Sat till 10:30

Madina Desi Curry BBQ €

An award-winning restaurant serving authentic South and North Indian cuisine. Vegetarians in particular will love the delicious curries such as their classic Aloo Gobi and Veg Korma as well as the various dhals and dosas (thin lentil pancakes, served with chutney and sambar) and warm Paratha flatbread straight from the oven.

🔲 190 C4 ✉ 60 Mary Street, D1
☎ 01 872 6007; www.madina.ie
🕐 Daily noon–11:30

Soup Dragon €

Tiny it may be, but Soup Dragon dishes up an imaginative and varied menu of fresh soups in three sizes. Good choices include Thai chicken and hearty mussel. They also serve delicious smoothies and a mean cup of coffee. You can even match a chunky soup with organic wine or beer. The cost of soup includes home-made bread and fruit. Ask about the occasional Souper Club, a four-course set menu.

🔲 1190 C3 ✉ 168 Capel Street North, D1
☎ 01 872 3277; www.soupdragon.com
🕐 Mon–Fri 8–5:30, Sat 10–4

The Winding Stair €€

Books, wine and great food are combined at the Winding Stair. The restaurant above the riverside bookshop serves dishes made with seasonal Irish ingredients, such as Lough Neagh brown trout or Kerry prawns served as a starter on toast with garlic and lemon. There are two sittings for dinner; the early sitting (6–8) attracts pre-theatre diners. Ask for a window table for views over Ha'penny bridge. **Insider Tip**

🔲 191 D4 ✉ 40 Ormond Quay Lower, D1
☎ 01 872 7320; www.winding-stair.com
🕐 Daily noon–10:30

Where to...
Shop

North of the Liffey shopping offers an authentic Dublin experience, with major department stores, markets and chain stores rather than the independent and sophisticated boutiques found on Southside.

DEPARTMENT STORES

Apart from **Brown Thomas** (➤ 117), you'll find most of Ireland's top department stores here. Some, including **Arnotts** in Henry Street (www.arnotts.ie) are unique to Dublin. Arnotts is Ireland's oldest and largest department store, full of fashions and childrenswear, with good beauty, interiors and sports departments too. The Homeware section stocks Irish products such as quality linen and Waterford crystal and cutlery and, if you start feeling peckish, there is an inexpensive cafe on the second floor and a popular restaurant on the top floor.

At Henry Street, **Debenham's** (www.debenhams.ie) has five floors of homeware and clothing. International designer John Rocha has joined forces with the store to create five exclusive collections – womenswear, menswear, childrenswear, accessories, and home – all at high-street prices.

MARKETS

Just off Henry Street, the Monday to Saturday **Moore Street Market**, selling fruit and veg, flowers, shoes and boots and bric-à-brac, has barely changed in decades. Something of a Dublin institution, it is worth seeing for local colour. Some pedlars still unload their wares from horse-drawn carts and **Insider Tip**

Northside

call out their prices in old Dublin dialects. In recent years immigrant traders have joined the throng to give the place a global vibe.

The chances are that horses may not be on your shopping list, but on the first Sunday of March and September, **Smithfield Square** stages a long-established horse market (► 132). The historic Smithfield area has long been a famous trading centre and was Dublin's main market venue from the Middle Ages until the late 1800s.

FASHION

In Jervis Street, the massive **Jervis Street Shopping Centre** (www.jervis. ie) is home to two floors of high-street stores and is Dublin's largest mall.

Penneys (tel: 01 872 0046) on Abbey Street is a good spot for disposable, fun fashion.

Close by, on the other side of Mary Street, **Ilac Centre** (www.ilac. ie) is Dublin's original shopping mall, with many of the popular chain stores represented; entrances are along Henry Street.

Among the stores in the chq Building on Custom House Quay is a branch of **Fitzpatricks Shoes** (5–6 chq Building, D1; www.fitz patricksshoes.com), one of the leading designer shoe stores in Ireland, with a selection of its own beautifully handcrafted shoes, and **Louis Copeland** (30 chq Building, D1; tel: 01 829 0409), originally Dublin's master tailor and now a men's outfitters selling its own brand of suits and shirts as well as various international brands.

Other stores in the chq Building include **Bunny's by the Bay** (7 chq Building, D1; tel: 01 672 0038) for cute baby clothes and soft toys. The stuffed toy bunnies, lambs and teddy bears (and more) are very well made and reasonably priced.

IRISH SOUVENIRS

The rejuvenation of Smithfield has included a new shopping centre on the site of an old medieval walkway called Duck Lane. It's a great place to shop for traditional Irish crafts.

For jewellery, **McDowell** (3 O'Connell Street Upper, D1; tel: 01 874 4961) specializes in traditional hand-crafted gold and silverware. Celtic metalwork was the pride of Ireland and many craftspeople are inspired by the designs on ancient chalices and ornaments. One of the most famous symbols, and a popular souvenir, is the Claddagh ring (the lovers' symbol of two hands cradling a heart and a crown).

BOOKS

Eason and Son (40 O'Connell Street, D1; www.easons.com) is the biggest bookseller in town, with a wide range of Irish literature and international newspapers.

MUSIC

Nearly all the top music shops are north of the river, including **Waltons** (2–5 North Frederick Street North, D1; www.waltons.ie) and **Goodwins** (134 Capel Street, D1; tel: 01 873 0846), which both sell fine hand-crafted *bodhrán* (pronounced "boran") drums, handmade harps, *uilléan* pipes and other traditional instruments that create the distinctive Irish sound. You'll also find a great range of sheet music.

FOOD

Cooks and foodies head to either **Moore Street Market** (► 141) or the **Epicurean Food Hall** (Liffey Street Lower, D1), with its galaxy of food shops selling specialities from around the world.

Where to...
Go Out

BARS & PUBS

Northside has some of the most stylish bars in town. The pricey **Morrison Bar** in Dublin's Morrison Hotel (➤ 46) is a top people-watching venue, created by John Rocha, Ireland's leading designer.

Bar Italia (26 Ormond Quay, D1; tel: 01 874 1000, www.baritalia.ie) serves home-made lasagna, tagliatelle and other Mediterranean classics. The tempting *dolci* (panna cotta or tiramisu) are definitely worth the indulgence and to end off – a strong shot of espresso.

The leading gay bar on the north side of the Liffey is **Pantibar** on Capel Street (7–8 Capel Street, D1; www.pantibar.com), with seven nights of parties, themed club nights and even movie screenings. The mood is a bit more mellow on Sunday evenings when it becomes an easy-listening chill-out for the party-weary.

Although there are fewer pubs north of the Liffey than on Southside, there are nevertheless some absolute corkers. **The Flowing Tide** (9 Abbey Street Lower, D1; tel: 01 874 4108), for instance, situated diagonally opposite the Abbey Theatre, is a popular watering-hole for the post-theatre crowd; every inch of the pub is covered in old and new theatrical posters.

As the Docklands makeover continues to take shape, so does the transformation of its pubs.

Topping the list here is the **Harbourmasters Bar** (IFSC Dock, D1, tel 01 670 1688; www.harbour master.ie), converted from the former harbour master's office into a traditional pub and restaurant overlooking the water.

The Green Room (Liffey Trust Centre, 117–126 Sheriff Street Upper, D1; tel: 01 894 4888, www. thegreenroombar.ie) is a wine and piano bar with a superb position next to the 3Arena (➤ 144), making it a convenient spot for pre- or post-concert drinks.

Further afield, good traditional pubs include **The Gravediggers** (Prospect Square, Glasnevin; tel: 01 830 7978), a eighth-generation, old-style pub (one of several in Dublin known as Kavanagh's) with a wonderful, almost countrified atmosphere. It serves one of the cheapest pints in town and is well worth the bus or taxi ride from the city centre. Situated at the gates of Glasnevin Cemetery (➤ 134), it earned its name during the days when grave diggers would slide a shovel through a hatch in the back wall of the pub as a tray to be filled with pints of Guinness.

Another good pub in the same area is the **Porterhouse Glasnevin** (Cross Gun's Bridge, Glasnevin; www.porterhousebrewco.com). The northern outpost of the Dublin-based microbrewery is one of the best places to try Irish stout and some of the company's award-winning lagers and ales. Why not try Wrasslers 4X (said to be Michael Collins' favourite beer), oyster stout (brewed with fresh oysters) or the extra strong Brainblásta? Like its city centre counterpart (➤ 86) this is a friendly, if noisy place, with plenty of seating. There is also an outdoor courtyard for warm summer evenings. Food is served, with the emphasis on affordable filling dishes.

LIVE MUSIC

Popular near the river is **The Grand Social** (35 Liffey Street Lower, D1; www.thegrandsocial.ie), which has four venues (the Parlour, the Ballroom, the Loft and the Garden), featuring a mix of live music, comedy and art.

Northside

Delivering a wide range of music throughout the week, **The Academy** (57 Middle Abbey Street, D1; www.theacademydublin.com) attracts international rock and pop bands, and there's also a room for DJs and dance acts. After 11pm from Wednesday to Saturday late-night clubs take over.

Over in The Docklands, the **Point Village** (www.pointvillage.ie) includes **3Arena** (www.3arena.ie), a major concert venue with capacity for 12,000 people. It hosts many of the city's headline-grabbing acts. Point Village (➤ 138) also incorporates a 220-room hotel and a 12-screen multiplex cinema.

Cobblestone Bar (77 King Street North, Smithfield Square, D7; www.cobblestonepub.ie) is the heart of traditional music in the Smithfield area, with some of the country's top session players often turning up for impromptu gigs.

The Knightsbridge Bar at the Arlington Hotel (23–25 Bachelor's Walk, D1; tel: 01 804 9100) has Irish music and dancing sessions at 9pm every night and at 5pm on Sunday afternoons.

Insider Tip

Further afield, the Irish music sessions at the 16th-century **Abbey Tavern** (tel: 01 832 2006; www.abbeytavern.ie) in the seaside suburb of Howth (➤ 168) are a Dublin institution and worth a trip on the DART. The Tavern has been going for over 200 years and its authentic interior is the ideal setting for an evening of Irish stew, Guinness and some traditional Irish music and dance. It can get very crowded, but even the tour groups do not detract from the pleasure of a night of Irish hospitality and music. On cold evenings the blazing peat fire, a strong Irish coffee and good company provide a warming welcome.

THEATRE

The north side of the Liffey has two of Dublin's most celebrated theatres.

Critics rate the productions at the **Gate Theatre** (Cavendish Row, D1; tel: box office 01 874 4045; www.gate-theatre.ie) as the best in Ireland. Founded in 1929, the Gate is known for its performances of modern Irish plays and its interpretations of popular international plays.

The Gate's great rival is the **Abbey Theatre** (Abbey Street, D1; tel: box office 01 878 7222; www.abbeytheatre.ie), which is internationally renowned for its productions of older Irish plays by such authors as Brendan Behan, Sean O'Casey, George Bernard Shaw, WB Yeats and JM Synge. The Abbey's smaller **Peacock Theatre** downstairs focuses on avant-garde works, providing a platform for work by emerging Irish talent.

CINEMA

The huge **Cineworld** (Parnell Street, D1; www.cineworld.ie) is one of the main cinemas in town. Round the corner, The **Savoy Cinema** (17 Upper O'Connell Street, D1; tel: 1520 927 004; www.imccinemas.ie) is one of the city's oldest cinemas, dating back to 1929. Now run by IMC Cinema, it has been converted into a modern six-screen cinema showing the latest blockbusters. The **Lighthouse Cinema Smithfield** (Market Square, D7; www.lighthousecinema.ie) screens an interesting mix of Irish, independent, foreign-language, arthouse and classic films.

COMEDY

Dubliners have a reputation for wit. The **Laughter Lounge** (4–6 Eden Quay, D1; www.laughterlounge.com) offers a feast of local and international stand-up talent (Thu–Sat). Performances start at 9pm and advance booking is advised. Many pubs also run occasional comedy evenings – keep an eye open for flyers.

Excursions

Excursions

A short distance outside Dublin, the beautiful Irish countryside offers a wealth of attractions from dramatic mountains and Celtic burial sites to stately homes and seaside villages. Most sights are within an hour's drive of the city and make ideal day and half-day excursions.

The counties immediately surrounding Dublin constitute the "Pale", the area of Ireland most strongly influenced in the past by English rule. Consequently, they are exceedingly rich in Anglo-Irish history, and brimming with abbeys, castles, churches and some of the country's finest stately homes. North of Dublin, in County Meath, the fascinating ancient passage tombs at Newgrange (➤ 152) are Ireland's most remarkable neolithic treasures. They are situated in the Boyne Valley, and the battle fought here (➤ 154), resulted in a landmark Protestant victory over the Catholics.

Closer to Dublin, head to the seaside for a fun day out. The coastline both north and south of Dublin is dotted with picturesque fishing villages, attractive towns, magnificent sweeping sandy beaches and rugged cliff-top walks, and provides plenty of opportunities for yachting, sailing, wind-

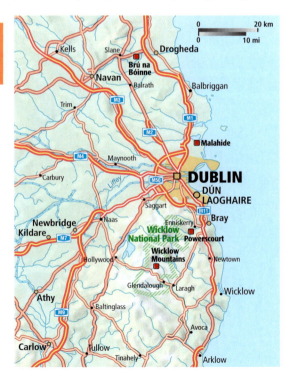

Baily Lighthouse at Howth Head

surfing and fishing. Two of County Dublin's most popular coastal villages are especially easy to reach by DART (➤ 42): picturesque Howth is beloved by locals and visitors for its seafood restaurants and breezy headland (➤ 168), while Malahide (➤ 151) is known for its medieval castle and its lively bars and pubs. To the south, the coastline is most spectacular beyond Bray, with Brittas Bay in County Wicklow possessing the best beach.

The capital's immediate hinterland is County Kildare, and the heart of Ireland's celebrated horse-racing country. The **National Stud** at Tully is well worth a visit to watch the horses being exercised and groomed.

Perhaps the most popular excursion from Dublin is to the heather moors and wooded glens of the Wicklow Mountains (➤ 148). This empty, rugged expanse of beautiful, untamed countryside is a walkers' paradise, and home to some impressive sights, including the evocative settlement of Glendalough, one of Ireland's most venerated monasteries, and the gardens of Powerscourt House (➤ 150).

Insider Tip

Getting Around

The best way to explore the lush countryside around Dublin is by car, although the DART north–south rail link provides easy access to many coastal suburbs. Alternatively, enjoy the countryside at a leisurely pace on a bicycle, or sit back and enjoy an organized tour. **Bus Éireann** (tel: 01 836 6111; www.buseireann.ie), **Wild Wicklow Tours** (tel: 01 280 1899; www.wildwicklow.ie) and **Gray Line Tours** (tel: 01 458 0054; www.grayline.com) all offer full-day tours to Newgrange and to the Wicklow mountains; **Dublin Bus** (tel: 01 873 4222; www.dublinbus.ie) arranges half-day coach tours of the north coast (including Malahide and Howth) and the south coast (including Killiney, Bray, Avoca and the Wicklow Mountains).

For the more energetic, consider walking the Wicklow Way with **Ireland Walk Hike Bike** (tel: 066 718 6181, www.irelandwalkhikebike.com) or a cycling weekend tour from Dublin to the Wicklow Mountains with **Irish Cycling Safaris** (tel: 01 260 0749; www.cyclingsafaris.com).

Wicklow Mountains

These rugged hills on Dublin's doorstep represent all that is best about the wild Irish landscape, with their lush glens, broad lakes and waterfalls, remote blanket bogs, bleak heather-clad heaths and dramatic peaks. Little wonder the Wicklow Mountains are one of the capital's favourite green lungs, filling the skyline to the south and enticing city-dwellers out at weekends to visit the "Garden of Ireland".

Few other capital cities live so close to a mountain range of such great size, variety and beauty as Dublin, with spectacular walks and views which begin just 17km (11mi) south of the city centre. Although the Wicklow peaks are small compared to the great mountain ranges of the world, they are high by Irish standards: **Lugnaquilla**, at 926m (3,038ft), is the country's 13th-highest peak.

Getting There

The main roads from Dublin into the Wicklow Mountains (via the Sally Gap, the Wicklow Gap or over Powerscourt Mountain) all offer striking viewpoints, but the real pleasure of this region is to go off the beaten track and explore the more remote corners of County Wicklow for yourself. Begin by taking the N81 Wexford road south from Dublin and turn left at Hollywood on the R756 to Glendalough.

Below left: Sally Gap in the mountains

Below centre: Gatehouse Archway at Glendalough

Glendalough

The area's main attraction is Glendalough – a ruined monastic settlement founded in the sixth century by the great misogynist and ascetic St Kevin, a member of the royal house of Leinster who became a recluse of the early Celtic church and built a contemplative cell in this deep, lovely valley in order to escape the sinful world. The site quickly became a major religious settlement in early Christian Ireland with a Europe-wide reputation for learning.

Today, Glendalough's remains include a perfectly preserved, 12th-century Round Tower (33m/108ft high), sturdy little chapels, a stone-built oratory and numerous Celtic crosses set against a magnificent mountainous back-drop. There are two lakes nearby – *Glendalough* means glen of the two lakes – and a well-maintained forest trail to the top end of the valley.

Ancient Stones

According to folklore, the **Athgreany Piper's Stones** – 14 prehistoric stones in a circle, with another just outside the formation – are the bodies of people turned to stone for dancing on pagan ground. The rock outside the ring is said to be the piper. They are located south of Blessington, on the road between Hollywood and Donard.

TAKING A BREAK

Stop at Ireland's highest pub, **Johnnie Fox's** (tel: 01 295 5647; www.jfp.ie), at Glencullen on the northern rim of the Wicklow Mountains. Undeniably touristy, it's celebrated for its fantastic seafood and traditional music sessions.

✉ Glendalough, County Wicklow (signposted from Kilmacanogue)
☎ 0404 45325 🕐 Visitor Centre: mid-Mar to mid-Oct daily 9:30–6; mid-Oct to mid-Mar daily 9:30–5
💶 Visitor centre: €4. Monastic site: free

INSIDER INFO

- Be sure to use a **good map** if you intend to walk in the Wicklow Mountains. Sheets 56 and 62 of the Irish OS 1:500,000 series cover the area in detail.
- The 132km (82mi) **Wicklow Way** stretches from Dublin over the Wicklow Mountains to Clonegal in County Carlow, starting just outside Dublin in Marlay Park. Contact the Irish Tourist Board for a pamphlet (▶ 174).
- The picture-postcard village of **Avoca** in the southern part of the Wicklow Mountains, better known to the world as "Ballykissangel", is something of a Mecca for fans of the popular British television series. The village also contains Ireland's oldest hand-weaving mill, the **Avoca Handweavers** (tel: 402 35105; www.avoca.ie) where you can purchase their beautifully woven fabrics

Powerscourt

The gardens at Powerscourt, just 25km (16mi) south of Dublin, are considered among the finest in Ireland, both for their exquisite design and for their magnificent setting in the Wicklow Mountains.

Powercourt is well worth the short drive from Dublin. To get there, take the N11 road south of Dublin, turn off at Enniskerry (south of Bray) and follow signs to Powerscourt.

The **gardens** were created in the mid-18th century, but re-designed in the 19th with planned gardens to the south and a series of formal rides and parkland to the north. Sweeping terraces link the house to the main lake and lead the eye onwards to the Sugar Loaf Mountain. The grounds are a blend of formal gardens, statuary and ornamental lakes, together with rambling walks, a walled rose garden and a pet cemetery. The land was granted to the First Viscount Powerscourt, Sir Richard Wingfield, by James I in 1609. Wingfield commissioned Richard Castle (1690–1751) to design a Palladian mansion around the shell of a 13th-century castle. In 1961 the Slazenger family (of tennis fame) bought the estate from the Ninth Viscount, and opened the gardens to the public. The **house** had just been restored when it was burned to a shell in 1974. Only the ballroom and garden rooms have since been restored. The remaining space has since been taken up with craft shops, the Terrace Café and a gift shop. The leaflet *A Walk Through Powerscourt Gardens* outlines three routes around the grounds.

Powerscourt **Waterfall**, at 121m (397ft) the highest in Ireland, is set in romantic landscape 6km (4mi) by car from Powerscourt Gardens.

Insider Tip

✉ Powerscourt Estate, Enniskerry, County Wicklow
☎ 01 204 6000; www.powerscourt.com 🕐 House: May–Sep Mon, Sun 9:30–1:30; Oct–Apr Sun 9:30–1:30. Gardens: Mar–Oct daily 9:30–5:30; to dusk rest of year ✋ House: €6.50. Gardens: €8.50. Waterfall: €5.50

Powerscourt House looks out over an elegant terrace and gardens

Malahide

The picturesque seaside village of Malahide is becoming an increasingly fashionable place to live. By the sea, near the airport, and just 14km (9mi) north of Dublin, it has excellent restaurants, lively pubs, chic boutiques, a smart new marina and Malahide Castle.

The huge and impressive castle stands in a large, wooded demesne. It remained in the hands of the Talbot family from around 1200 until 1976, except for a brief interlude during the rule of Oliver Cromwell (1653–58). A guided tour of the interior reveals the castle's transition from a simple medieval fortress to a stately home of fairy-tale appearance, complete with turrets and towers. Most of the furnishings are Georgian, in keeping with the castle's decor, and some of the National Portrait Collection is housed in the castle's grand banqueting hall, including portraits of various Talbot family members.

The castle grounds provide opportunities for walking and picnicking, and the **Talbot Botanic Gardens**, created by the late Lord Milo Talbot between 1948 and 1973, are well worth visiting. The **Fry Model Railway** is the largest such display in the world. The huge collection of handmade model trains and trams from the beginning of rail travel to the present day will be exhibited in the Malahide Casino. (The casino is undergoing restoration, and is due to be opened to the public sometime in 2017.) **Tara's Palace Childhood Museum** (www.childhoodmuseum.org) in Powerscourt House (➤ 150) has a unique doll's house as its centrepiece. The miniature masterpiece was handcrafted and painted by renowned Irish craftsmen and artists.

Insider Tip

Malahide Castle – one of Ireland's oldest such buildings

✉ Malahide, County Dublin   🚌 42   🚆 DART train to Malahide

Castle
☎ 01 816 9538; www.malahidecastleandgardens.ie
🕐 Daily 9:30–4:30   🎫 €12, children: €6

Brú na Bóinne

The tranquil 15km (9mi) stretch of lush farmland at Brú na Bóinne (a bend in the Boyne) in County Meath, 53km (33mi) north of Dublin, marks the cradle of Irish civilization. Today it boasts Europe's richest concentration of ancient monuments – forts, henges, standing stones and the mysterious grand passage tombs of Newgrange, Dowth and Knowth.

This fertile river valley was first settled during the Stone Age and soon became the most important settlement in the country. The Brú na Bóinne Visitor Centre helps to interpret the neolithic monuments in an extensive exhibition, including a full-scale replica of the chamber at Newgrange and a model of one of the tombs at Knowth.

Getting There
Take the N1 Belfast road out of Dublin to Drogheda, then follow signs to Brú na Bóinne, on the L21 4km (2.5mi) north of Donore village

Newgrange
The spectacular passage grave at Newgrange is, without doubt, the high point of a visit to Brú na Bóinne, staggering for its sheer size and complexity of construction, and containing the greatest concentration of megalithic art in all Europe. This massive, grassy tumulus, measuring 85m (280ft) in diameter and more than 10m (30ft) high, dates from around 3000BC. Its exterior walls are faced with brilliant white quartzite resembling a giant kerbstone. The sophisti-

cated entrance, with its large, mysteriously carved Threshold Stone, is constructed with a narrow slit like a letterbox. It would seem that the chamber had a significance beyond that of a burial place as, once a year on the morning of the winter solstice, the rays of the sun flood through this slit and illuminate the interior.

A guide leads you by torchlight along a 19m (62ft) passage to the beehive-shaped central burial chamber, to marvel at the intricate patterns of the wall carvings. When Newgrange was excavated, only a handful of bodies were found. Nobody understands the reason, but it would appear that the funerary remains were regularly removed – perhaps once the sun had taken the spirits of the dead with it, after the winter solstice.

Newgrange is just one of around 40 burial sites within this celebrated bend in the Boyne. Nearby are the mounds of **Dowth**, 3km (2mi) east of Newgrange (visible from the road); **Knowth**, 1.5km (1mi) northwest of Newgrange, with its magnificent megalithic tomb art; and various other strange tumuli, some of which have not yet been excavated.

Slane

It's not just Newgrange that makes the Boyne Valley so celebrated. Indeed, it was on the nearby Hill of Slane that, in AD344, St Patrick is said to have kindled the flame of Irish Christianity. According to legend, the druids were celebrating their feast day on the Hill of Tara, but before they could ignite their sacred fire, Patrick had prepared his Easter feast and had lit his Paschal fire at Slane. The Druids, having seen the flames, warned High King Laegaire that if Patrick's fire were not extinguished, it would burn forever in Ireland.

Passage grave, Newgrange

Battle of the Boyne

The Boyne Valley returned to prominence on 1 July, 1690 (11 July in our modern calendar) at the Battle of the Boyne. Having been deposed in 1688, the Catholic ex-King of England, James II, rallied the support of French and Irish Catholics, and challenged his successor, the Protestant King William of Orange, at Oldbridge on the banks of the Boyne. A bloody battle ensued. The Protestants triumphed and James fled to France, marking the start of Protestant power in Ireland. Mention of this feud still fuels Catholic and Protestant passion – not so much about the battle as about what it represents: the difficulty of building a common future.

Ruins of **Slane's old abbey on the Hill of Slane**

Brú na Bóinne
✉ Visitor Centre, Donore, County Meath (2km/1mi west of Donore village, south side of River Boyne) ☎ 041 988 0300; www.heritageireland.ie
🕐 Daily Mar–Apr 9:30–4:30; May–Sep 10–5; Oct–Feb 9–4
✋ Newgrange: €6; Knowth: €5; combined ticket: €11, Visitor centre only: €3

Battle of the Boyne
✉ Visitor Centre, Oldbridge, Drogheda, County Meath
☎ 041 980 9950; www.battleoftheboyne.ie
🕐 Tours by pre-booking only, daily

INSIDER INFO

- Access to Newgrange and Knowth is by **guided tour only**. Tickets cannot be bought in advance, so arrive early. Be prepared for delays during summer months.
- The **last tour** of the monuments leaves the Visitor Centre one hour and 45 minutes before the site closes.
- The simulated **solstice experience** at the replica Newgrange burial chamber is well worth doing. There is a 10-year waiting list of people wanting to experience the real phenomenon!

Walks

1 VIKING & MEDIEVAL DUBLIN

Walk

DISTANCE 3.2km (2mi)   **TIME** 1.5 hours
START/END POINT Dublin Castle, Dame Street, D2 ✚ 190 C2
🚌 3, 27, 40, 49, 54A, 77A, 123 (Dame Street),
9, 14, 15, 15A, 15B, 16, 65, 65B, 83, 122 (Georges Street)

This walk combines Dublin's castle and cathedrals with some of the lesser-known historic sights. It's best done on a Sunday, when there's less traffic and the peal of church bells helps to create a more "medieval" atmosphere.

❶–❷

Start at **Dublin Castle** (➤ 70), the heart of the historic city and the site of the *Dubh Linn* (Black Pool), where the Vikings once moored their longboats. Leave the castle via the main entrance, passing the Georgian **City Hall** (➤ 76) on your right. Turn right on to the main street. The traffic lights here mark the site of Dame Gate, one of the principal gateways to the walled medieval city, long since demolished. Turn left down Parliament Street, then left again into a narrow street called Essex Gate, where a small bronze plaque on a stone pillar (on the right) marks the original site of Essex Gate, another former entrance to medieval Dublin.

❷–❸

To your right, Exchange Street Lower follows the curve of the walls. It used to be called Blind Quay, because the city

The Brazen Head pub on Lower Bridge Street

walls obscured views of the river. Continue along Essex Street West, which, in common with many of the lanes here, has been called various names over the centuries, including Stable Lane, Smock Alley and Orange Street. Soon you will reach **Fishamble Street**.

❸–❹

In the 10th century, Fishamble Street was the main thoroughfare from the Viking port to the High Street, the principal trading street. It takes its name from the fish stalls or "shambles" that once lined its streets. In 1742, Handel conducted the premiere of his *Messiah* in a music hall here, performed by the joint choirs of St Patrick's and Christ Church cathedrals. A plaque at the entrance to the **George Frederic Handel Hotel** commemorates the event. From here, head downhill towards the Liffey. Before you turn left into Wood Quay, on your right

is Betty Maguire's celebrated *Viking Boat* sculpture. Continue along Wood Quay, past the modern **Civic Offices** (▶ 160) built in the late 1970s by Dublin Corporation on top of the old Viking settlement.

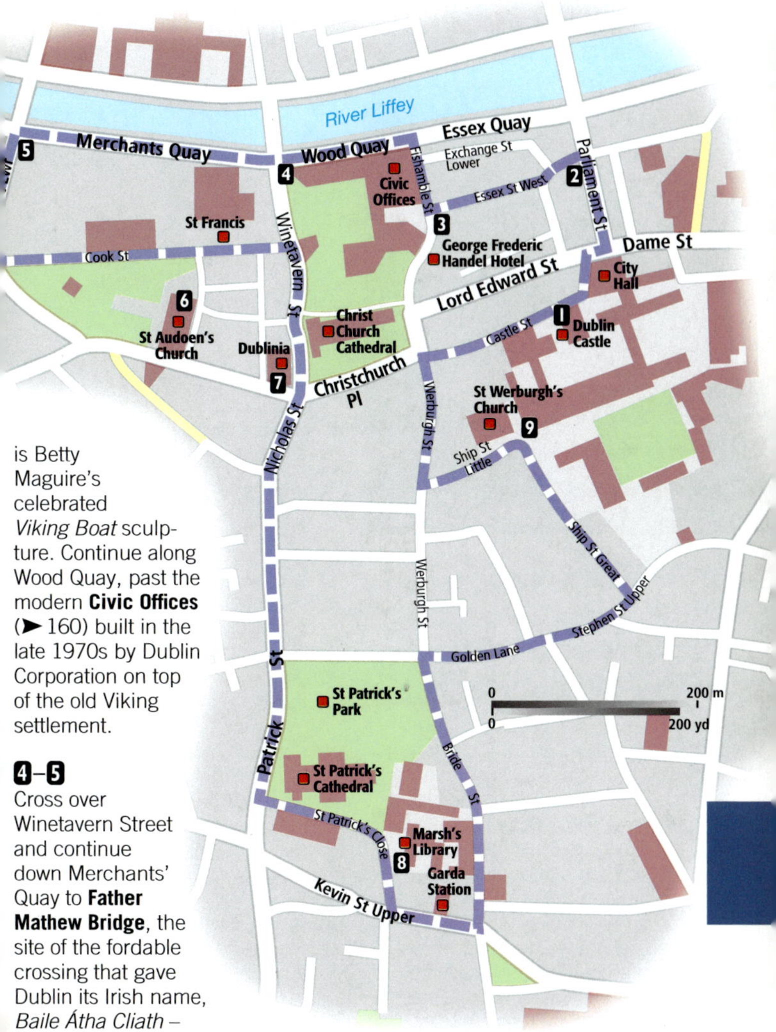

4–5

Cross over Winetavern Street and continue down Merchants' Quay to **Father Mathew Bridge**, the site of the fordable crossing that gave Dublin its Irish name, *Baile Átha Cliath –* "Town of the Hurdle Ford".

5–6

Turn left up Bridge Street Lower past Dublin's oldest pub – the **Brazen Head** (▶ 86) – dating from 1198 (although the current building is 17th-century). Turn left again into Cook Street. The large section of fortified wall here is a mainly reconstructed version of the original city wall built around 1100. The street is named after the cooks who had to prepare food outside the city as most of the buildings, and even the walkways, were made of wood and highly inflammable.

Insider Tip

TAKING A BREAK

Try **Leo Burdock's** (▶ 81) for the best fish & chips, or **Chez Max** (▶ 80) for a French meal.

Walks & Tours

Looking through St Audoen's Gate

Halfway along on your right, St Audoen's Gate – Dublin's only remaining medieval gateway – leads to **St Audoen's** Protestant church (▶ 74), the city's only surviving medieval parish church.

6–**7**

Continue along Cook Street, past the **Church of St Francis** on your left. It is more commonly called the "Adam and Eve" church, after a former tavern here that concealed a secret chapel during the days of Penal Law in the 18th century. Turn right up Winetavern Street to **Christ Church Cathedral** (▶ 76), the city's oldest building and the mother church of Dublin. It is joined to **Dublinia** (▶ 75), a museum of medieval Dublin, by a covered bridge, which was added to the cathedral during major reconstruction in the 1870s.

7–**8**

Cross over the major junction at Christchurch Place and proceed down Nicholas Street to St Patrick's Park, where the saint is said to have baptized some of the first Irish Christians in a well. Next door to the park is **St Patrick's Cathedral** (▶ 65), founded in 1191 on the site of an earlier wooden church outside the walls. The level of its entrance (in St Patrick's Close) is 2m (6ft) lower than the modern street – at the original level of the medieval city. Halfway along St Patrick's Close is **Marsh's Library** (▶ 78), the oldest public library in Ireland.

8–**9**

Turn left into Kevin Street Upper. The **Garda Station** on the left occupies the Episcopal Palace of St Sepulchre, home of the archbishops of Dublin from the late 12th century until 1830 when the Dublin metropolitan police took possession. Turn left into Bride Street, then fourth right into Golden Lane where the facades of some buildings incorporate scenes from *Gulliver's Travels* (below), in honour of Jonathan Swift, the Dean of St Patrick's (▶ 20 and 67). Take the left fork into Stephen Street Upper, then first left into Ship Street Great, behind Dublin Castle, where there is a section of the old city wall at the sharp left bend in the street.

9–**①**

Turn right into Werburgh Street. The tall spire of St Werburgh's Church on the right was dismantled in 1810 because the authorities feared snipers might use the site to fire into Dublin Castle. Turn right into Castle Street. From here it's a short walk back to the entrance of Dublin Castle.

THE LIFFEY
Walk

DISTANCE 3.2km (2mi)   **TIME** 1.5 hours
START POINT Heuston Station ✚ 187 D5
END POINT Pearse Station ✚ 192 C2

The Liffey has always been Dublin's nerve centre and its main artery, neatly bisecting the city from west to east. To walk along its banks provides a fascinating insight into the city's maritime history, from its Viking origins to the latest modern dockland developments.

1–2

Start at **Heuston Station**, Dublin's most impressive train station, and one of Europe's finest. Named after Seán Heuston, a rebel of the 1916 Easter Rising, the building bears the date 1844, even though a stonemason's strike delayed its completion until 1848. Cross the Liffey to the Northside, over the yellow **Frank Sherwin Bridge** (1982), and proceed along Wolfe Tone Quay – named after the father of Irish Republicanism (► 21), past Collins Barracks, now home

to the Decorative Arts & History branch of the **National Museum** (► 129), on your left. The **Guinness Brewery** is on the opposite bank. It once had its own jetty here, from which 10 purpose-built Guinness barges set out along Ireland's inland waterways to distribute their "black gold".

2–3

Continue on the north bank past **Rory O'More Bridge** (1863), the start point for the Liffey Swim in September and Mellowes Bridge (1768), then cross over the 1818 Father Mathew Bridge (► 157). In Viking times the river here was around 250m (820ft) wide. On the corner, **O'Shea's Merchant pub** is celebrated for its live traditional music. Opposite lies Dublin's oldest pub – the **Brazen Head** (► 86).

Bachelors Walk along the River Liffey

Detail of the friezes on Sunlight Chambers in Parliament Street

3–4

Proceed along Merchant's Quay, with its grand view of the **Four Courts** (► 133) on the opposite bank. Designed by English-born architect James Gandon with a Corinthian portico and copper-covered lantern dome, it is considered by many to be one of the finest 18th-century public buildings in Dublin.

Insider Tip

4–5

Pass O'Donovan Rossa Bridge (1816) and the monstrous green-house-like **Civic Offices** of the Dublin Corporation on Wood Quay,

built in the 1970s on an important Viking site and received with dismay by most Dubliners, who dubbed them "the bunkers". On the corner of Essex Quay and Parliament Street stands **Sunlight Chambers**, a turn-of-the-20th-century building with painted terracotta friezes advertising the company's product – soap. The bridge here was first erected in 1678 by Sir Humphrey Jervis, a nobleman who was developing land on the north side of the river in order to connect his properties advantageously to the castle. It was rebuilt in its present form in 1753, modelled on Westminster Bridge in London and named Grattan Bridge after Henry Grattan, the leader of the old Irish Parliament. Cross over the bridge, glancing behind you at the magnificent classical facade of the **City Hall** (► 76) at the top of Parliament Street.

5–6

Continue eastwards along the smart wooden boardwalk, constructed in 2000, which runs parallel to **Ormond Quay** and is dotted with small coffee bars. The quays on the north bank of the Liffey date mostly from the

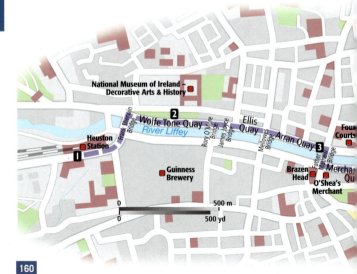

National Museum of Ireland – Decorative Arts & History

Wolfe Tone Quay

Ellis Quay

Arran Quay

Four Courts

Heuston Station

River Liffey

Frank Sherwin Bridge

Rory O'More Bridge

James Joyce Bridge

Mellowes Bridge

Father Mathew Bridge

Merchant Quay

Guinness Brewery

Brazen Head

O'Shea's Merchant

Merchant

0 500 m
0 500 yd

late 17th century and were laid out in graceful irregularity. **These buildings were Dublin's earliest merchant houses, and those along Ormond Quay are particularly attractive.** *Insider Tip* On the opposite bank, the tall narrow houses of Wellington Quay provide an almost continental feel. This was the last city quay to be built, in 1812. Its most celebrated structure is the **Clarence Hotel** (► 44). Upstream from the Clarence, the River Poddle, the main waterway of medieval Dublin, joins the Liffey through an opening in the quay wall. There was a harbour here until 1625, making Temple Bar Dublin's busiest trading area, and the Clarence was once the Custom House. However, as the average tonnage of vessels increased the docks were forced to move further east.

6–7

The next bridge – the **Millennium Bridge** (1999) – is solely pedestrian, linking Northside with Temple Bar. Alongside it, a second pedestrian-only bridge – **Ha'penny Bridge**

(1816) – is one of the oldest cast-iron structures of its kind in the world. It derived its name from the toll charged to cross it for more than 100 years. Opposite the bridge, look out for the sculpture *Meeting Place* by Jakki McKenna in Liffey Street – two shoppers on a bench, nicknamed "The Hags with the Bags".

7–8

O'Connell Bridge (1880) marks the end of the boardwalk and also the finishing line of the Liffey Swim. Continue eastwards and just before Butt Bridge (1932) look out for the immense building known as **Liberty Hall**, at 16 storeys the highest building in Dublin and the second highest in Ireland. Cross over the road to the **Custom House** (► 136), the highlight of Dublin's Georgian heritage.

8–9

Cross the road to see the sculpture group of emaciated people – *Famine Figures* – by Rowan Gillespie,

Walks & Tours

TAKING A BREAK
Several pubs and restaurants line the Liffey: The Winding Stair (▶ 141), above a tiny bookshop, has views over Ha'Penny Bridge.

created in memory of the Great Famine of 1845–49. Turn back and head up Memorial Road and into Amiens Street. Turn first right into the Custom House Docks, the area that replaced Temple Bar when the new Custom House and its adjoining dock basins were opened in 1791. They, too, were abandoned in the early part of the 20th century – the era of even larger ships – but in 1987 rejuvenation of the area commenced with the development of the Financial Services Centre. The water is a central feature of this new district. Walk past the Harbourmaster's Bar, cross a small bridge and look left into the **Inner Dock**, an area of major residential development.

9–**10**

Turn right on to George's Dock, where the **chq Building**, filled with cafes and shops, occupies and updates "Stack A", once a tobacco warehouse and still among the world's finest remaining examples of 19th-century industrial architecture. Head past an antique, hand-operated crane down towards the Liffey and the restored **Scherzer Bridges** (1912), which regulate the entrance to the docks.

10–**11**

Cross the Liffey via Sean O'Casey Bridge, looking left to see the spectacular Samuel Beckett Bridge, built by renowned Spanish architect Santiago Calatrava and opened in 2009. On the south side of the river is the **Seaman's Memorial**, a large anchor commemorating the 13 Irish merchant ships and their crews lost in World War II – a high number considering the small fleet and the neutral position of Eire. Beyond lies the deep-water docks and the sea. Sir John Rogerson's Quay, which runs eastwards from here, was neglected for decades but is now undergoing radical redevelopment (overseen by the Dublin Docks Development Authority), with shops, hotels, pubs, restaurants and apartments.

11–**12**

From the Seaman's Memorial it is a short walk down Lombard Street East to Pearse Station.

The Ha'penny Bridge reflected in the waters of the River Liffey

3 PUB CRAWL
Walk

DISTANCE 1.6km (1mi)   **TIME** Depends on your thirst!
START POINT Mulligan's, Poolbeg Street, D2 ✚ 192 B4;
get there from Tara Street, DART Station
END POINT Toner's, 139 Baggot Street Lower, D2 ✚ 188 B4

"Good puzzle would be to cross Dublin without passing a pub," mused Leopold Bloom in James Joyce's novel *Ulysse*s, and the task proves just as difficult today. Dublin is world famous for its pubs and the city is awash with them. With more than a thousand to choose from, this "crawl" takes you to some of the best – for beer, for atmosphere, for music, for literary associations, and for good *craic* (➤ 36).

1–2
Start the pub crawl at **Mulligan's** (➤ 119) in Poolbeg Street. Not only is it among the city's most famous pubs, but it also serves one of the best pints of *Guinness* in Dublin. The interior is rough and ready and it's usually pretty noisy; the elaborate Victorian pub frontage is also one of Dublin's finest. To reach Mulligan's, turn left out of Tara Street DART Station and walk along George's Quay. Take the first left then the first right into Poolbeg Street.

2–3
After Mulligan's, return to the quay-side and proceed to the O'Connell Bridge. Turn left down Westmorland Street and right into Fleet Street. The old **Palace Bar** (➤ 85) here was a popular haunt for journalists and writers in the mid-20th century. The front bar is long and narrow, while the back of the pub feels more like a living room than a pub.

The Oliver St John Gogarty in Temple Bar

3–4
Go further along Fleet Street into Temple Bar where you will be spoilt for choice of watering holes. Try **The Oliver St John Gogarty** (➤ 86), the **Temple Bar** (➤ 86) or The Norseman (➤ 85). Continue to Parliament Street where the modern, lively **Porterhouse** (➤ 86) brews its own porter, ale and lager.

4–5
Head up Parliament Street. Turn left at the traffic lights into Dame Street, first right down South Great George's Street, then first left into narrow Dame Lane to the **Stag's Head**. This attractive, country-style pub, named after the stuffed and mounted stags' heads on its walls, has original Victorian mirrors, lamps and stained-glass windows

(pictured ➤ 165 top), and a
magnificent bar topped with red
Connemara marble. The lunches
here are excellent too.

5–6

Continue to the end of Dame Lane,
bear right into Trinity Street, and
left into St Andrew Street. Ahead
of you on the corner opposite
Dublin Tourism is the mock-Tudor,
half-timbered facade of **O'Neills**,
on the corner of Church Lane
and Suffolk Street, one of the
most boisterous pubs in the city –
a hugely popular student haunt
with five bars, just a stone's throw
from Trinity College.

6–7

Proceed down Suffolk Street towards Trinity College and turn
right into Grafton Street. A clutch
of good pubs lies just off Grafton
Street. In Wicklow Street **The
International,** renowned for its
jazz and comedy nights, and the
Old Stand (opposite, in Exchequer
Street) are meeting places for
rugby fans before an international
match. In Duke Street **Bailey**
(➤ 119), with its long literary
traditions, vies for custom with
Davy Byrne's (➤ 119), celebrated
for its Joycean connections. In
Anne Street South there's **Kehoe's**
(➤ 119), a genuine old-style pub
with traditional decor, intimate
surroundings and excellent *craic*,
while **McDaid's** (➤ 120) in nearby
Harry Street is a must for Behan,
O'Brien and Kavanagh fans.

    Neary's (also called the **Chatham
Lounge**), just off Grafton Street on
Chatham Street, is a popular haunt
of actors from the nearby **Gaiety
Theatre** (➤ 120). You'll find a
comforting atmosphere, a well-
worn interior, creamy pints of porter
and friendly bar staff there.

7–8

At the end of Grafton Street, turn
left along the edge of St Stephen's

Green North then first left up
Dawson Street. Almost immediately
on your left is the **Dawson Lounge**
(No 25), Dublin's smallest pub.
==Be sure to arrive early to get
a space at the bar.== **Insider Tip**

8–9

Continue along St Stephen's Green
North, past **The Shelbourne Hotel**
(➤ 46). A little further down the
street, on Merrion Row,
you'll find
O'Donoghue's
(➤ 119), Dublin's
most famous
music pub where
the folk group The
Dubliners began
their musical career
around 40 years
ago. If you're lucky,
you may find an im-
promptu traditional
music session in full swing.

9–10

Continue straight on into Baggot
Street Lower, the location of cosy,
antique-style **Doheny & Nesbitt**
(➤ 119) with its fine mahogany
bar – a favourite after-work haunt
for the lawyers, journalists and
politicians who work in this area,
but surprisingly devoid of tourists.
Nearly opposite, **Toner's** (➤ 119)
is another wonderfully traditional
19th-century pub, complete with
a snug, ancient mirrors and old-
fashioned drawers that were once
used for storing tea and other
groceries. Toner's is allegedly
the only pub that WB Yeats ever
entered. Yeats was brought here
by his friend, the local surgeon
Oliver St John Gogarty, who lived
in nearby Ely Place. Yeats sat in
the snug just inside the door,
politely sipped his glass of sherry,
then rose swiftly, saying to
Gogarty, "I have seen a pub now,
will you kindly take me home?"
Toner's marks the end of this
pub crawl.

Stained glass window in
the Stag's Head pub

River Liffey

George's Quay

1 Tara
Street
Station

2 Mulligan's
Poolbeg St

Tara St

3 Palace
Bar

Fleet St

Temple Bar

**Temple
Bar**

**Oliver
St John
Gogarty**

Westmoreland St

O'Connell Bridge

Burgh Quay

Trinity College

St

Dame

Lane

O'Neill's **6**

Suffolk St

St Andrew St

5 **Stag's
Head**

Exchequer St

**Old
Stand**

International

Wicklow St

0 — 200 m
0 — 200 yd

Bailey

Duke St

Davy Byrne's

Grafton St

Kehoe's

Anne St South

McDaid's

Dawson St

Neary's

**Gaiety
Theatre**

**The Dawson
Lounge**

7 **8**

St Stephen's Green North

Merrion Row

**Doheny &
Nesbitt**

9

O'Donoghue's

St Stephen's Green

Baggot St Lower

Toner's

10

Beer pumps at the
Long Hall Pub

4 GEORGIAN DUBLIN
Walk

DISTANCE 2km (1mi)   **TIME** 1 hour
START/END POINT St Stephen's Green ✚ 191 E1
🚌 10, 11, 13, 14, 14A, 15A, 15B

Dublin treasures its Georgian past and this walk, around three of the city's five Georgian squares, highlights some fine architecture, as well as noting the quirkier features of the period.

❶–❷
St Stephen's Green is one of the landmarks of the Georgian city and **Newman House** (➤ 106), designed in 1739, was the first stone-faced house on the Green. Set off from here, heading eastwards along the south side of the Green, past splendid **Iveagh House** (➤ 106). At the southeastern corner, glance to your right up Earlsfort Terrace to the **National Concert Hall**, Ireland's foremost classical concert venue.

❷–❸
Cross over and continue straight ahead up Leeson Street Lower. The third turning left into Pembroke Street Upper leads to **Fitzwilliam Square**, the smallest and last of Dublin's five Georgian squares to

be completed, but arguably the best preserved, and the only Georgian square whose park is still reserved for residents. Notice the doorways painted in bright colours (pictured below), and such original details as anti-burglar spikes set in the walls.

❸–❹
Walk around the south and east sides of the square, keeping the park railings on your left, then head up Fitzwilliam Street. This impressive thoroughfare was known as the Georgian Mile as it contained the longest stretch of uninterrupted Georgian town-house architecture in Europe – until the 1960s, that is, when an outrageous piece of civic vandalism allowed the construction of a hideous modern office building to house the Electricity Supply Board. Ironically, that same company has completely restored the Georgian mansion next door at No 29, converting it into a museum (➤ **Number Twenty Nine**, 112).

❹–❺
By now you have reached the southeastern corner of **Merrion Square** (➤ 111), one of Dublin's grandest squares. To your right is the late Georgian **St Stephen's Church** in Mount Street Upper, fondly known as the Pepperpot because of its unusual dome. In Georgian times, the Grand Canal behind the church would have been a bustling waterway of commerce.

Georgian Dublin

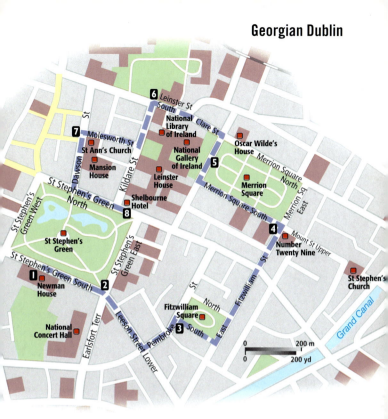

4–5

Turn left along the south side of Merrion Square. Look closely at the buildings to see a wide variety of decorative fanlights above the doors, wrought-iron balconies on the upper floors, and boot-scrapers and coal-hole covers outside each house. At weekends, the railings of Archbishop Ryan Park, in the square, are hung with paintings by hopeful artists looking for a sale. **Leinster House** (➤ 110) and the **National Gallery of Ireland** (➤ 101) dominate the western side of Merrion square.

Insider Tip

5–6

Leave Merrion Square by the northwest corner. On the opposite corner, **No 1** (➤ 111), was the home of Oscar Wilde from 1855 until 1878. Continue along Clare Street and the southern edge of Trinity College.

6–7

Turn left down Kildare Street, past the **National Library of Ireland** (➤ 110) and Leinster House, then take the second right into Molesworth Street, where three early Georgian houses with curvaceous gables and huge chimneys are known as the **Dutch Billies**.

7–8

Turn left down Dawson Street, past **St Ann's Church** (➤ 109) and Queen Ann-style **Mansion House**, home of the Lord Mayor. At St Stephen's Green, turn left and cross Kildare Street to **The Shelbourne Hotel** (➤ 46 and 116).

TAKING A BREAK
Indulge in a high tea at **The Shelbourne Hotel** (➤ 116) on St Stephen's Green.

5 HOWTH HEAD
Walk

DISTANCE 11km (7mi)   **TIME** Minimum 4 hours
START/END POINT Howth DART Station ✚ 185 off F4
🚆 DART to Howth (24 minutes from the city centre).

A bracing stroll around the coastal promontory of Howth Head, with its dazzling 360-degree views over the city, Dublin Bay, and the hills and coastline for 50km (30mi) around is, without doubt, the most spectacular walk on the north side of Dublin. It also provides a perfect respite from the hurly-burly of the city centre.

❶–❷
Turn left out of Howth's DART station, past the harbour full of fishing boats. The **waterside** is dotted with fishmongers and little restaurants, and you may even catch a glimpse of a seal in the water as the vessels unload the day's catch.

❷–❸
Turn right up Abbey Street. Climb the steps on the right beside **Ye Olde Abbey Tavern** to reach the ruins of **St Mary's Abbey** (above),

once a medieval seat of learning famed throughout Europe, now little more than a roofless 16th-century shell. The view from here over Howth Marina (picture ➤ 170) and the crooked, crab-like claws of the harbour break-waters is sensational. Howth (rhyming with "both") takes its name from the Norse word *Hoved* meaning "head". The peninsula was an island until comparatively recent times when an isthmus of gravel formed, thereby connecting it to the mainland.

❸–❹
Go down Church Street back into Abbey Street and take the next right up St Lawrence's Road. After 100m, continue along Grace O'Malley Road, then left up Grace O'Malley Drive. Follow this as it bends right, then left alongside some woods. At No 37, continue straight ahead along a path that

rejoins the road. Continue for 20m, then turn up the steps beside Robin Hill House.

4–5

Turn right at the top, and go up a ramp beside Ballylinn (No 53). Ascend a grassy slope, keeping to the right for a little way, and then up the steep slope through the trees. Turn right and keep the rugby pitches well to your left and the golf course to the right, until you are parallel with the top of the golf course.

HIDDEN TREASURE

The knobbly white quartzite rocks ringing Shielmartin's crown were placed here 2,000 years ago to mark the burial place of Crimhthan Niadhnair, warrior king of Ireland. Helped by his goddess wife, Nar of the Brugh, he mounted attacks on the newly arrived Romans in Britain, returning home laden with plunder. No one knows where the king buried his booty: some say it's on Shielmartin, others claim it lies on the promontory under the Baily Lighthouse.

Walks & Tours

5–6

Bear right around the top edge of the golf course, following the path into trees. Cross the next golf course, Howth Golf Course (keeping a good look-out for flying golf balls), and climb the slope ahead. This steep, rough path, flanked by dense purple heather, leads to the top of **Shielmartin**. At 171m (561ft), this is the highest point on the peninsula. Pause for a while to enjoy the views: to the south is Dublin Bay, the city and the Wicklow Mountains beyond; to the north is the scenic coastline of Portmarnock, Lambay Island and Ireland's Eye, and, on a clear day, the distant Mountains of Mourne.

6–7

A clear path leads from here southwards down to **Carrickbrack Road**. Turn left, and 300m later cross the road and pass through a kissing gate (by the "Dangerous Cliffs" sign). This path leads through rocks down to the shoreline.

7–8

Turn left and follow the narrow, rocky cliff path for 8km (5mi) all the way round Howth Head, past the **Baily Lighthouse**, admiring the sensational seascape of deep-cut coves, lichen-clad stacks and stumps, bracken-covered slopes and hedgerows of fuchsia and gorse. **Howth Head** boasts more than half the total of Ireland's indigenous plant species and an abundance of wildlife and seabirds. Remember also James Joyce and *Ulysses*. It was here that Leopold Bloom proposed to Molly "the day we were lying among the rhododendrons on Howth Head in the grey tweed suit and his straw hat, the day I got him to propose to me, yes…"

8–9

Continue along the coastal path back into Howth. As you turn the corner at the **Nose of Howth**, your efforts will be rewarded by breathtaking views of the northern coastline and Ireland's Eye. This weathered islet was once a monastic settlement but nowadays only seabirds live here. In summer there are regular boat trips here from Howth Harbour.

9–10

Return along the coastal path to Howth, then back down to the harbour and the DART station.

Organized Tours

On Foot

Dublin is compact and easy to explore on foot. Here are some of the best organized walking tours.

The **Historical Walking Tour of Dublin**, led by Trinity College history students, provides an excellent introduction to the city – a guide to its cultural, religious and political history, exploring such key events as the influence of the American and French revolutions, the Potato Famine of 1845–48, the 1916 Rising and the Northern Ireland peace process. Another self-guided option is to download one of 11 themed tours of Dublin from www.visitdublin.com to an iPod or MP3 player. The "iWalks" include Castles and Cathedrals, In the Steps of Ulysses and Dalkey to Sandycove, looking out over Dublin Bay (tel: 01 605 7700; www.visitdublin.com/iwalks).

Perhaps the best way to get a feel for the city's alcohol-fuelled literary heritage is to try a **Literary Pub Crawl**, where two actors perform recitations and anecdotes from Joyce, Beckett, Yeats, O'Casey, Behan, Lavin and Wilde between visits to four of the pubs made famous by these writers. A great combination of street theatre, Guinness and *craic!*

In a similar vein, the **Musical Pub Crawl** is led by two professional musicians who perform tunes and songs while telling the story of Irish music, between visits to famous musical pubs such as The Oliver St John Gogarty (➤ 86) and culminating in a musical *seisiún*.

If modern music is more your style, try the self-guided **Rock 'n' Stroll Trail** which takes in such venues as O'Donoghue's, the Bad Ass Café (where Sinéad O'Connor once waitressed), Merchant's Arch (where Phil Lynott played in his pre-Thin Lizzy days) and the Windmill Lane recording studios, made world famous by U2. Call into Dublin Tourism in Suffolk Street (➤ 41) to pick up a booklet.

If you're feeling brave, try the **Haunted History Tour**, a unique tour with members of the PSI Ireland (Paranormal Study and Investigation). The tour visits scenes of murder and intrigue in the elegant surrounds of Georgian Dublin and you are introduced to the works of famous writers who excelled in horror, the supernatural and the bizarre.

By Bus

Hop-on hop-off tours of the city centre give an excellent overview of Dublin and are a convenient means

Walks & Tours

of sightseeing, with stops near most of the major attractions. Each bus has a tour guide who delivers a witty and informative commentary, and your day ticket enables you to hop on and off as often as you wish. Look out for red City Sightseeing buses, green-and-cream Dublin City buses, and black-and-gold Gray Line buses.

Dublin boasts the world's only **Ghostbus**. This is no ordinary tour. The blood-red curtains inside the bus are drawn closed to ward off evil spirits lurking outside and those on board are transported to the spooky side of the fair city, far removed from the tourist attractions of daytime Dublin. Actors bring the ghosts, fiends and phantoms of the city's troubled past to life, with highlights including Count Dracula's Dublin origins, torch-lit body-snatching in St Kevin's graveyard and a visit to the steps of St Audoen Protestant church, reputedly haunted.

On the Water

Sea Safari takes you on a high-speed, adrenalin-packed tour in a rigid inflatable boat around Dublin Bay and the coastline from Skerries to Killiney Bay, with possible sightings of seals, porpoises and other wildlife along the way.

Viking Splash Tours aboard a yellow, reconditioned World War II amphibious vehicle take you from land to water to see the city sights. Children love it…especially the big splash into the Grand Canal Basin.

Ghostbus Tour
✉ Start: Dublin Bus, 59 Upper O'Connell Street, D1; duration: 2 hours
☎ 01 703 3028; www.dublinsightseeing.ie ⏰ Mon–Thu 8pm, Fri, Sat 7pm, 9:30pm 💶 €28

Haunted History Tour
✉ Start: The Small Square (next to City Hall on Dame Street), D2; duration: 1.5–2 hours
☎ 085 102 3646 (booking essential); www.hiddendublinwalks.com ⏰ Mon, Thu, Sat 8pm 💶 €13

Historical Walking Tour of Dublin
✉ Start: Trinity College (front gate), D2; duration: 2 hours ☎ 087 688 9412; www.historicaltours.ie
⏰ May–Sep daily 11, 3; Apr, Oct daily 11; Nov–Mar Fri–Sun 11 💶 €12

Hop-on Hop-off Bus Tours
✉ Start: 14 O'Connell Street, D1; duration: 1.5–1.75 hours
☎ 01 898 0700; www.loveireland.com ⏰ 9:30–5:30 💶 €18

Literary Pub Crawl
✉ Start: Upstairs at the Duke pub, 9 Duke Street, D2; duration: 2 hours
☎ 01 670 5602; www.dublinpubcrawl.com
⏰ Apr–Oct daily 7:30pm; Nov–Mar Thu–Sun 7:30pm. Arrive by 7pm! 💶 €12

Musical Pub Crawl
✉ Start: Upstairs at the Oliver St John Gogarty pub, Fleet Street, D2; duration: 2.5 hours
☎ 01 475 3313; www.discoverdublin.ie
⏰ Apr–Oct nightly 7:30; Nov, Feb–Mar Thu–Sat 7:30pm 💶 €12

Sea Safari
✉ Start: Convention Centre, North Quay, D1; duration: 1 hour ☎ 01 668 9802; www.seasafari.ie
⏰ Daily noon, 2pm and 4pm 💶 €20

Viking Splash Tours
✉ Start: St. Stephen's Green North; duration: 1.5 hours ☎ 01 707 6000; www.vikingsplash.ie
⏰ Mid-Feb to Dec: 10 tours per day 💶 €20, children: €12

Practicalities

Practicalities

WHAT YOU NEED

● Required
○ Suggested
▲ Not required
△ Not applicable

Entry requirements differ depending on your nationality and are also subject to change without notice. Check prior to a visit and follow news events that may affect your situation.

	UK	USA	Canada	Australia	Ireland	Netherlands
Passport/National Identity Card	●	●	●	●	▲	●
Visa (waiver form to be completed)	▲	▲	▲	▲	▲	▲
Onward or Return Ticket	▲	▲	▲	▲	▲	▲
Health Inoculations	▲	▲	▲	▲	▲	▲
Health Documentation (➤ 178, Health)	○	●	●	●	●	●
Travel Insurance	○	○	○	○	○	○
Driving Licence (national/international)	●	●	●	●	●	●
Car Insurance Certificate (if using own car)	●	△	△	△	●	●
Car Registration Document (if using own car)	●	△	△	△	●	●

WHEN TO GO

☐ High season   ☐ Low season

JAN	FEB	MAR	APR	MAY	JUN	JUL	AUG	SEP	OCT	NOV	DEC
8°C	8°C	10°C	13°C	15°C	18°C	20°C	19°C	17°C	14°C	10°C	8°C
46°F	46°F	50°F	55°F	59°F	64°F	68°F	66°F	63°F	57°F	50°F	46°F

☀ Sun   ⛅ Sunshine and showers   🌧 Wet   ☁ Cloudy

Temperatures are the **average daily maximum** for each month. The best time to visit Dublin is between April and October, when the weather is at its best, although the city is popular to visit at any time of year. **Peak tourist months** are July and August; book accommodation early. Christmas and the New Year are also popular. During November to March, the weather can be changeable; most of the time it is cloudy, and frequently wet, dark and dreary. Autumn is generally fine, with a high percentage of crisp days and clear skies. Be prepared for rain at some time during your stay, no matter when you visit, but try to accept the rain as the Irish do – as a "wet blessing".

GETTING ADVANCE INFORMATION

Websites
■ www.visitdublin.com
■ www.ireland.com
■ www.dublinstemplebar.com
■ www.indublin.ie
■ www.timeout.com/dublin

Tourist Offices In Dublin
Dublin Tourism Centre
Suffolk Street, D2
☎ 01 605 7700

GETTING THERE

■ **By Air** There are **direct scheduled flights** from Britain, mainland Europe and North America to Dublin Airport (tel: 01 814 1111; www.dublinairport.com). The Republic's national airline is **Aer Lingus** (tel: 0871 718 5000 (UK); 1890 800 600 (Ireland); www.aerlingus.com). **Other scheduled carriers** include American Airlines, Delta, British Airways, British Midland, Air France, Alitalia, Iberia, Lufthansa and SAS. **Ryanair** (tel: 0871 246 0000 (UK); 0818 303 030/01 249 7791 (Ireland); www. ryanair.com) offers cheap rate fares from destinations around Europe. For **current flight details** of all main carriers, services, ticket prices, special offers and packages, check with your travel agent, the airlines or the internet.

Approximate flying times to Dublin: from the UK (1–2 hours), from mainland Europe (2–4 hours), from USA/Canada (6–9 hours), from Australia/New Zealand (12-plus hours).

■ **By Ferry** Ferries from the UK sail into Dublin and Dun Laoghaire, 14km (9mi) south of the city. **Irish Ferries** (tel: 08705 171717 (UK); 0818 300 400 (Ireland); www. irishferries.com) operates daily between Dublin Port and Holyhead (1 hour 50 minutes by fast ferry; just over 3 hours by cruise ferry). Their MV *Ulysses*, the world's largest car ferry, has capacity for 2,000 passengers, and a crossing time of just over 3 hours between Dublin Port and Holyhead.

P&O Ferries (www.poferries.com) and **DFDS Seaways** (www.dfdsseaways.co.uk) operate daily services between Dublin and Liverpool; journeys take seven hours.

Stena Lines (tel: 08447 570 7070 (UK); 01 204 7777 (Dublin); www.stenaline.ie) operates a daily fast service (99 minutes) between Dun Laoghaire and Holyhead, or a 3.5-hour crossing from Dublin Port to Holyhead.

TIME

Ireland runs on **Greenwich Mean Time (GMT)** in winter. From late March until late October, clocks are put forward 1 hour, and British Summer Time (GMT +1) operates.

CURRENCY & FOREIGN EXCHANGE

Currency The monetary unit of the Republic of Ireland is the Euro (€). Notes are in denominations of €5, €10, €20, €50, €100, €200 and €500, and coins in denominations of €1 and €2, and 1, 2, 5, 10, 20 and 50 cents.

Travellers' cheques are the most convenient way to carry money. All major credit cards are widely recognized.

Exchange Most banks and bureaux de change will exchange cash and travellers' cheques.

Banks tend to offer better exchange rates than store, hotels and bureaux de change, although the latter generally stay open later than banks. You will find booths at the airport, sea ports, some department stores and some railway stations. Many banks have ATMs for cash withdrawal.

TOURISM IRELAND: www.tourismireland.com

In the UK
103 Wigmore Street
London W1U 1QS
☎ 0800 039 7000

In the USA
345 Park Avenue
New York, NY 10154
☎ (212) 418-0800

In Australia
5th Level
36 Carrington Street
Sydney, NSW 2000
☎ 02 9299 6177

Practicalities

NATIONAL HOLIDAYS

1 Jan	New Year's Day
17 March	St Patrick's Day
March/April	Good Friday/Easter Monday
First Mon May	May Holiday
First Mon June	June Holiday
First Mon Aug	August Holiday
Last Mon Oct	October Holiday
25 Dec	Christmas Day
26 Dec	Boxing Day

Each region also observes an Anniversary Holiday.

ELECTRICITY

 The power supply is 240 volts AC. Sockets generally are the UK type, with three square pins. Overseas visitors should bring a voltage transformer and plug adaptor.

OPENING HOURS

- ○ Shops
- ● Offices
- ● Banks
- ● Main Post Offices
- ● Museums/Monuments
- ● Pharmacies

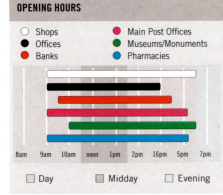

8am 9am 10am noon 1pm 2pm 16pm 5pm 7pm

☐ Day ☐ Midday ☐ Evening

Shops Some shops open on Sun. Late-night shopping (8pm) is Thu.
Banks Most close Sat. Some open till 5pm Thu.
Pharmacies These display a list of pharmacies open at night and on Sundays. O'Connell's Late Night Pharmacy, 55 O'Connell Street Lower, is open Mon–Fri 7:30am–10pm, Sat 8am–10pm, Sun 10–10.

TIPS/GRATUITIES

Most restaurants now include a service charge, so a tip is not necessary, although it is customary to round up the bill, leaving an extra 5 per cent of the total.

Restaurants (service not included)	10%
Bar service	No
Taxis	10%
Tour guides	€1
Porters	50 cents
Chambermaids	Discretion
Lavatories	Small change

PARKING

There is a pay-and-display system in the city centre and car parks along Parnell Street, Dawson Street, Drury Street, Fleet Street and Abbey Street and at the IFSC in the Docklands north of the Liffey. A few hotels have free parking for guests or charge a daily fee.

TIME DIFFERENCES

Dublin (GMT)	London (GMT)	New York (EST)	Los Angeles (PST)	Sydney (AEST)
12 noon	12 noon	← 7am	← 4am	→ 10pm

STAYING IN TOUCH

Post Post offices and vans are painted green. Post offices are open Mon–Fri 9–5:30, Sat 9–1. The General Post Office on O'Connell Street is open Mon–Sat 8–8, Sun 10–6.

Public Telephones Public phone booths are grey or green-and-white, and take coins, credit cards or phone cards (sold at post offices and newsagents).

For national telephone enquiries, dial 11811. For other countries, dial 11818. For national operator assistance, dial 10. For the international operator, dial 114.

All numbers preceded with 1800 are toll-free.

International Dialling Codes Dial 00 followed by:

UK:	44
USA/Canada:	1
Ireland:	353
Australia:	61
Germany:	49
Spain:	34

Mobile providers and services Most GSM phones can be used in Ireland but check with your provider that you have a roaming agreement before leaving home and be clear about costs. It might be cheaper to buy a GSM sim card and pay for calls at the local rate, or if you're staying for more than a month, to buy a cheap "pay as you go" phone and top up when necessary. The main companies are Vodafone, Three, Meteor and Tesco Mobile.

WiFi and Internet These are available at the airport and in many hotels. Some hotels charge a fee but the majority are free. There are also plenty of internet cafes (► 179) and some ordinary cafes that offer free WiFi to attract customers.

PERSONAL SAFETY

Until recently, street crime was rare in Dublin, but petty crime is now on the increase. To be safe:

- Keep watch of handbags and wallets in public places.
- Use your hotel safe.
- At night, avoid Phoenix Park, poorly lit alleys and side-streets.
- Keep cars well secured and avoid leaving property visible inside.
- The national police are called **Garda Siochána** (pronounced shee-*kaw*-nah) and wear black-and-blue uniforms.
- If you are a victim of crime contact the nearest police (Garda) station, where staff will contact **ITAS** (Irish Tourist Assistance Service; **www.itas.ie**).

Alternatively go direct to ITAS. Their volunteers offer free advice:
✉ 6–7 Hanover St East, D2
☎ 01 890 365 700
🕐 Mon–Fri 10–6
or
✉ Store St Garda Station, D2
🕐 Sat 10–6, Sun noon–6

Police assistance:
☎ 999 or 112 from any phone

POLICE	999 or 112
FIRE	999 or 112
AMBULANCE	999 or 112

Practicalities

HEALTH

 Insurance Nationals of EU and certain other countries can get medical treatment at reduced cost with the European Health Insurance card (not required by UK nationals). Medical insurance is essential for all other visitors.

 Dental services EU nationals, or nationals of other countries with which Ireland has a reciprocal agreement, can get dental treatment within the Irish health service with the European Health Insurance card (not needed for UK nationals). Others should take out private medical insurance.

 Weather June and July are the sunniest months, although July and August are the hottest. If visiting at these times, cover up and apply a good sunscreen.

 Medication Pharmacies are easily recognized by their green cross sign. Their highly qualified staff are able to offer medical advice on minor ailments, provide first-aid and prescribe a wide range of over-the-counter drugs.

 Safe Water Tap water is safe to drink. Mineral water is widely available, but often expensive.

CONCESSIONS

Senior citizens (over 60) are entitled to discounts on transport and most admission fees on proof of age. **Students** under 18 are entitled to reduced entrance in some museums and galleries. Be sure to carry some form of identification. Holders of an International Student Identity Card can buy a **Travelsave Stamp** which entitles them to travel discounts including 50 per cent reduction on the Irish bus and train network (Bus Éireann and Iarnród Éireann), and Irish Ferries between Britain and Ireland. Contact your local student travel agency for further details. The Travelsave Stamp can be purchased from USIT, 19–21 Aston Quay, O'Connell Bridge, D2 (tel: 01 602 1906).

TRAVELLING WITH A DISABILITY

Helpful information is available from the National Disability Authority at 25 Clyde Road, Dublin D04E409 (tel: 01 608 0400; www.nda.ie) and from the Irish Wheelchair Association (24 Blackheath Drive, Clontarf, D3; tel: 01 818 6400, www.iwa.ie).

CHILDREN

Many sights, museums and attractions offer reductions. Baby-changing facilities are excellent in the newer museums. Special attractions are marked out in this book with the logo shown above.

RESTROOMS

Public facilities are usually clean and safe. Most galleries and museums have lavatories, and most bars, fast food outlets and stores will let you use theirs.

CUSTOMS

EU: 800 cigarettes/400 cigarillos; 10L spirits; 90L wine; 110L beer. **Non-EU:** 200 cigarettes/ 100 cigarillos, 1L spirits, 4L wine, 16L beer and goods to the value of €430 (€215 if under 15 years old).

EMBASSIES & HIGH COMMISSIONS

UK
☎ 01 205 3700

USA
☎ 01 668 8777

New Zealand
☎ 01 660 4233

Australia
☎ 01 664 5300

Canada
☎ 01 234 4000

The Irish Language

Irish Gaelic (*Gaelige*) is the Republic's official language, and is commonly referred to as "Irish". Closely related to the Gaelic languages of Scotland, Wales and Brittany in France, Irish remained the country's language right up to the time of the Great Famine. In Dublin today, Irish is spoken by some and understood by many, but English predominates.

The past decade has seen a resurgence of interest in the Irish language. It can be studied at Trinity College and several other universities; children are taught it throughout their school days, and must sit an examination in it as part of their leaving certificate.

USEFUL WORDS & PHRASES

Yes / No **Sea / Ní hea**
Hello **Dia dhuit**
Goodbye **Slán agat/Slán leat**
Please **Más é do thoil é/Le do thoil**
Thank you **Go raibh maith agat**
Today / Tomorrow **Inniu / Amárach**
My name is… **…is ainm dom**
How much does it cost? **An mó atá air?**
Where is…? **Cá bhfuil…?**
Hotel **Óstan**
Restaurant **Bialann**
Menu **Biachlár**
Beer **Beoir**
Wine **Fíon**
Lavatories **Seomra folctha**
Entrance / Exit **Bealach isteach / Éalú**
Open / Closed **Oscailte / Dúnta**

Monday **Dé Luain**
Tuesday **Dé Máirt**
Wednesday **Dé Céadaoin**
Thursday **Dé Déardaoin**
Friday **Dé Haoine**
Saturday **Dé Sathairn**
Sunday **Dé Domhnaigh**

NUMBERS

One **Aon**
Two **Dó**
Three **Trí**
Four **Ceathair**
Five **Cúig**
Six **Sé**
Seven **Seacht**
Eight **Ocht**
Nine **Naoi**
Ten **Deich**
Twenty **Fiche**
Thirty **Tríocha**
Forty **Daichead**
Fifty **Caoga**
One hundred **Céad**
One thousand **Míle**

Internet Cafes

Central Internet Cafe
✉ 6 Grafton Street, D2
☎ 01 677 8298; www.centralinternetcafe.com
🕐 Mon–Fri 7am–11pm, Sat 9am–10pm, Sun 10am–8pm

Xtreme Internet Centre
✉ 30–31 Liffey Street Lower, D1
☎ 01 873 0965
🕐 Daily 9am–11pm

World Link Call Shop
✉ 79a Talbot Street, D1
☎ 01 855 2560; www.worldlink.ie
🕐 Mon–Fri 9–9; Sat 10–6, Sun 11–6

CLONE IRL
✉ 6 Lower Ormond Quay, D1
☎ 01 872 8479; www.cloneirl.com
🕐 Mon–Fri 10–7; Sat noon–6; closed Sun

Recommended Reading

The Irish literary tradition is one of the most illustrious in the world. Dublin has produced three Nobel Prize winners, and many other writers of international renown. Below is a selection of books written about Dublin as well as some of the most popular fictional and biographical works by Dubliners and set in the city:

BOOKS ON DUBLIN

Douglas Bennett *An Encyclopaedia of Dublin* (Gill & Macmillan, Ireland). Everything you could ever want to know about the capital.

Maeve Binchy *Dublin 4* (Poolbeg). Four short stories observing the decadent lifestyle of the D4 district south of the Liffey.

Max Caulfield *The Easter Rebellion* (Gill & Macmillan, Ireland). The definitive guide to the events of 1916.

Peter Costello *Dublin Churches* (Gill & Macmillan, Ireland). An illustrated record of more than 150 churches.

John Cowell *Dublin's Famous People: Where They Lived* (O'Brien Press). Brief biographies of local luminaries.

Maurice Craig *Dublin 1660–1860* (Liberties Press). An historical account of an evolving city.

Terry Deary *Dublin* (Horrible Histories Gruesome Guides). An engaging children's guide that reveals all the gory secrets of Dublin's historic streets and buildings.

Frank Hopkins *Hidden Dublin* (The Mercier Press). Subtitled Deadbeats, Dossers and Decent Skins, this book explores "backstage Dublin" from poverty to weird and wonderful exploits.

Deirdre Purcell *Follow Me Down to Dublin* (Hodder Headline Ireland). Memories of old Dublin.

Colm Quilligan *Dublin Literary Pub Crawl* (Writers Island). The accompanying book to the tour of pubs with literary links.

BOOKS SET IN DUBLIN

Brendan Behan *Borstal Boy* (Arrow). A romanticized biography, portraying the author's involvement in the Republican movement and his early years in prison.

Dermot Bolger *Father's Music* (Flamingo). A psychological thriller set in Dublin.

Christy Brown *My Left Foot* (Minerva). This is an unsentimental autobiography of Christy Brown, who was born with cerebral palsy, in which he describes his life as part of a large Southside family.

Philip Casey *The Fabulists* (Lilliput). A compelling love story set in contemporary Dublin.

Roddy Doyle *The Commitments* (Minerva), *The Snapper* (Penguin), *The Van* (Penguin). A witty trilogy centred on the north Dublin Rabbitte family written in a vernacular style.

James Joyce *Ulysses* (Penguin). An epic account of 24 hours in the life of hero Leopold Bloom, set in Dublin, at the same time drawing parallels with Homer's Odyssey.

Iris Murdoch *The Red and the Green* (Penguin). A fictional account of an Anglo-Irish family during the Easter Rising.

OTHER NOTABLE WORKS BY DUBLINERS

Samuel Beckett *Molloy, Malone Dies, More Pricks than Kicks* and *The Unnameable*
Brendan Behan *The Hostage*
Maeve Binchy *Circle of Friends, The Lilac Bus* and *Light a Penny Candle*
Roddy Doyle *A Star Called Henry*
James Joyce *Portrait of the Artist as a Young Man*
Bram Stoker *Dracula*
Jonathan Swift *Gulliver's Travels*
Oscar Wilde *The Picture of Dorian Gray*

Street Atlas

For chapters: See inside front cover

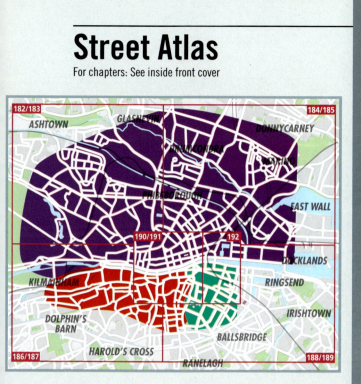

Key to Street Atlas

🛈	Information	〰	(Swimming) beach	
Ⓜ	Museum	⚠	Youth Hostel	
🎭	Theatre Opera house	🐘	Zoo	
● LUAS Tram	LUAS Tram		Public building	
◀ARROW◀	Railway		Notably building	
DART	DART suburban railway		Pedestrian precinct	
⚑	Monument		Water	
✝ ✡	Church / Synagogue		Park area	
📖	Library		Forest	
★	Point of Interest			
⛺	Lighthouse	190–192	Detailed city map	
⌣	Golf course			
✿ ✉	Police station / Post office	★	TOP 10	
✚	Hospital	26	Don't Miss	
🅿	Car park	22	At Your Leisure	
⚓	Marina			

1 : 22.000

0	500	1000 m
0	500	1000 yd

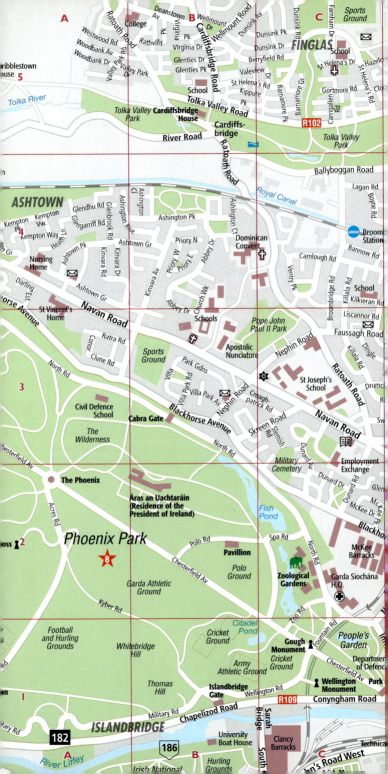

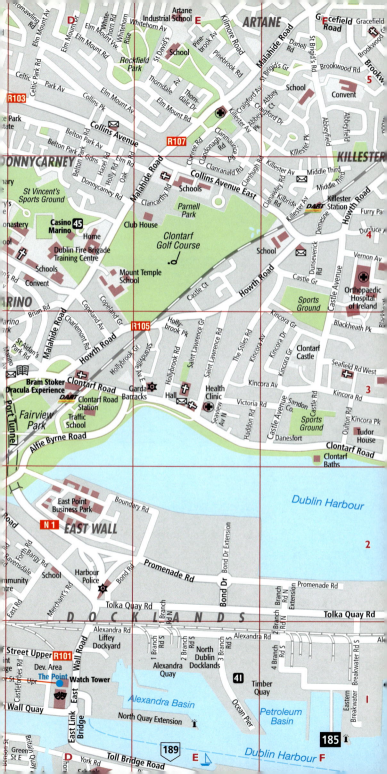

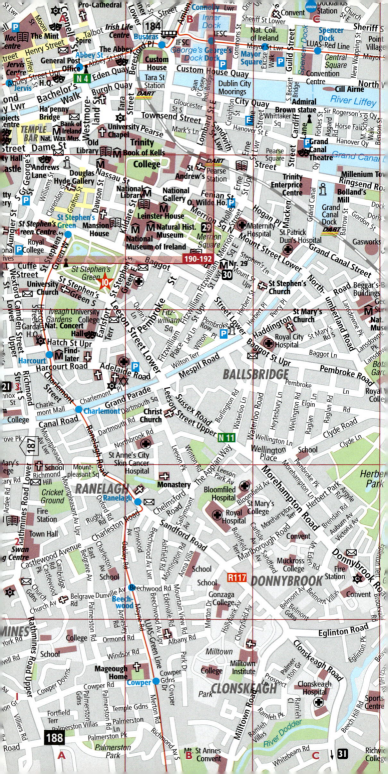

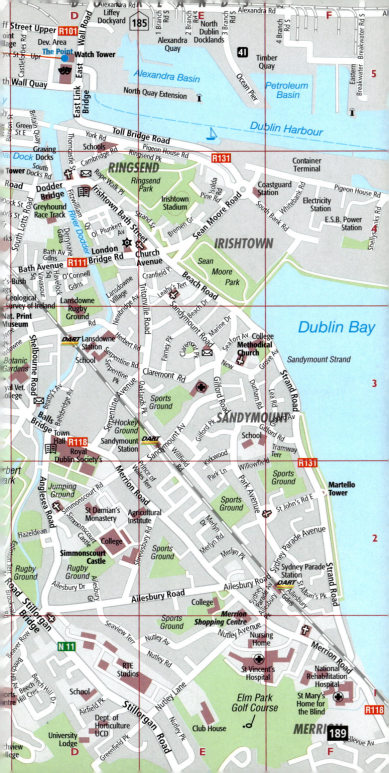

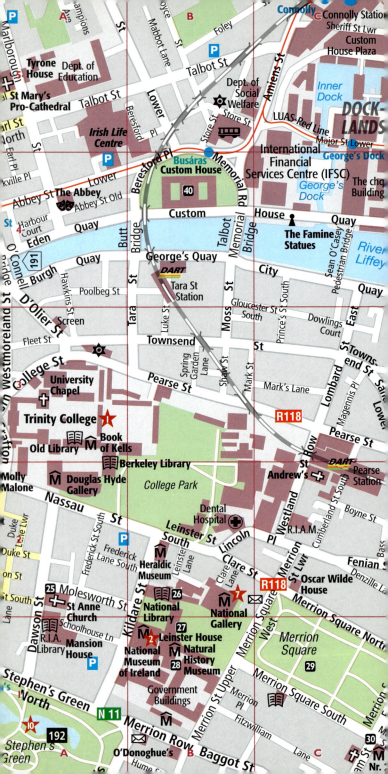

Street Index

Street Index

Street Index

Index

Index

Picture Credits

Credits

1st Edition 2017

Worldwide Distribution: Marco Polo Travel Publishing Ltd
Pinewood, Chineham Business Park
Crockford Lane, Chineham
Basingstoke, Hampshire RG24 8AL, United Kingdom.
© MAIRDUMONT GmbH & Co. KG, Ostfildern

Authors: Teresa Fisher, Louise McGrath, Dr. Manfred Wöbcke
Editor: Isolde Bacher (text_dienst)
Revised editing and translation: Margaret Howie, www.fullproof.co.za
Program supervisor: Birgit Borowski
Chief editor: Rainer Eisenschmid

Cartography: © MAIRDUMONT GmbH & Co. KG, Ostfildern
3D-illustrations: jangled nerves, Stuttgart

Printed in China

Despite all of our authors' thorough research, errors can creep in. The publishers do not accept any liability for this. Whether you want to praise us, alert us to errors or give us a personal tip – please don't hesitate to email or post to:

MARCO POLO Travel Publishing Ltd
Pinewood, Chineham Business Park
Crockford Lane, Chineham
Basingstoke, Hampshire RG24 8AL
United Kingdom
Email: sales@marcopolouk.com

FSC
www.fsc.org
MIX
Paper from
responsible sources
FSC® C124385

10 REASONS
TO COME BACK AGAIN

Leabharlanna Poiblí Chathair Bhaile Átha Cliath
Dublin City Public Libraries

 A **Guinness** in Davy Byrne's in Dublin quite simply tastes better than in any Irish pub at home.

 Singing Irish **folk songs** with complete strangers in Dublin's pubs will make you want to return.

 Almost any time is the right time for an **Irish coffee** in one of Grafton Street's many cafes and pubs.

 In Dublin there is no **bad weather**, only bad clothing – so take your Wellington boots!

 The original **brown soda bread** served at breakfast is good enough to keep you coming back.

 You need another visit to see more of the city's vibrant and colourful **Georgian doors**.

 The **Wicklow Mountains** are full of mystical places and ancient mansions waiting to be explored.

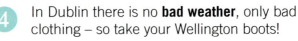 You will get to know another **poet** with each visit – either in literature or in person.

 Knitwear, tweed, pottery – Ireland is the place to buy **souvenirs**, and there is always more to buy.

10 Ask a Dubliner for directions just so you can hear the lovely **Irish brogue**, something that you'll never tire of hearing.